W9-CHZ-680

drawnandquarterly.com

First edition: February 2017
Printed in China
10 9 8 7 6 5 4 3 2 1

Library and Archives Canada Cataloguing in Publication
Bagge, Peter, author, illustrator
*Fire!! The Zora Neale Hurston Story* / Peter Bagge.
ISBN 978-1-77046-269-4 (hardback)
1. Hurston, Zora Neale—Comic books, strips, etc. 2. African American women novelists—Biography—Comic books, strips, etc. 3. African American women authors—Biography—Comic books, strips, etc. 4. Women folklorists—United States—Biography—Comic books, strips, etc. 5. Graphic novels I. Title.
PS3515.U789B34 2017 813'.52 C2016-904672-9

Published in the USA by Drawn & Quarterly, a client publisher of Farrar, Straus and Giroux. Orders: 888.330.8477

Published in Canada by Drawn & Quarterly, a client publisher of Raincoast Books. Orders: 800.663.5714

Published in the United Kingdom by Drawn & Quarterly, a client publisher of Publishers Group UK. Orders: info@pguk.co.uk

PETER BAGGE

DRAWN + QUARTERLY

## FRONT COVER

This is a composite of several photographs of Hurston at the start of her first anthropological field trip in 1927. In preparing to travel the back roads of her native Florida, Hurston blew through most of her research grant almost immediately by equipping herself with a new car, a Stetson hat, and a six-shooter "for protection." Her brother Bob feared the gun would invite more trouble than it would prevent, but all it did was invite curious stares, particularly in the way its holster contrasted with her white sundress.

In fact, in the ensuing years and countless miles spent crisscrossing the South, Hurston never ran into any serious trouble, with the law or anybody else, which could be attributed to her (literally) disarming personality.

## BACK COVER

While promoting her newest book in Chicago in 1934, Hurston ran into her friend, portrait photographer Carl Van Vechten. He convinced her to pose for countless photographs, which included the only known full color photographs of Hurston. This drawing is based on one of the color photos, in which she's wearing what Van Vechten described as a "traditional Norwegian skiing outfit." (Hurston had a well-deserved reputation for being an adventurous dresser.)

Though apprehensive at first, Hurston was thrilled when Van Vechten sent her prints of the results. In response she wrote to him: "I love myself when I am laughing, and then again when I am looking mean and impressive"—a line that Alice Walker used as the title of a Hurston reader, which she edited in 1979.

# WHY HURSTON

TRY AS I MIGHT, I CAN'T RECALL THE CIRCUMSTANCES that led to me reading *Their Eyes Were Watching God* twenty or thirty odd years ago. It certainly wasn't a homework assignment, since I was already way too old for that. And the subject matter—the evolution of a poor Black woman living in the South in the early twentieth century—was hardly something I figured I'd relate to. I just simply recall hearing or reading that it was "really good," so I bought it or borrowed it from someone.

And like many readers, at first I struggled with the thick, outdated regional dialect the book was written in, though after a while I got used to it, and soon was perpetually amazed at how fluid, rhythmic, and lyrical that dialect was. It was an endless cascade of metaphors and similes: some profound, others just plain old hilarious. Did people really talk like this back then? Well, Zora Neale Hurston did!

I quickly followed that up by reading Hurston's autobiography (and along with *Their Eyes*, her best known book), *Dust Tracks on a Road*. Not only did I find it equally engaging, but in this instance I actually did find myself relating to her—at least insofar as her attitude toward life, art, and politics were concerned. She clearly was an iconoclast and independent speaker, one who took great pains to make her thoughts and opinions as clear as possible, since her views—especially her political views—did not fall easily on the usual left/right binary political spectrum.

While Hurston was obviously all in favor of freedom and equal opportunity for anyone of any gender or race to speak their minds and live their lives as they saw fit (and indeed, that's what her own life was all about), she was equally determined to pursue her achievements on her own terms, without letting anyone else confine her or dictate the context and terms she wrote in. Her determination to go her own way was so profound that she often sounded like she was being contrary for its own sake. In fact, her first biographer, Robert Hemenway, speculated that this was out of spite, in response to her feeling ostracized by her left-leaning peers—and, living and working in an academic bubble himself, he also seemed to wonder if she was mentally ill!

The biggest irony of Hurston's life was how she (along with her contemporary Langston Hughes) practically defined what later became known as the "Black Pride" movement. At first subconsciously, she soon became willfully determined to celebrate all aspects of African-American life, to see and preserve the art and beauty in all of it. Yet this warts-and-all approach is the very thing that brought her criticism from most of her Black peers—particularly mentors like Alain Locke and W. E. B. Du Bois, who were obsessively conscious of the white gaze. To them, her willingness to include pimps and whores, street hustlers, and illiterates in her stories (not to mention her insistence in not only including but even narrating in a lower class, backwoods dialect) would only confirm white racist assumptions (as if white racists in the 1930s eagerly purchased books written by Black authors, but I digress).

The other great divide between her and her Black artist peers was the latter's near-universal buy in of leftist economic theories: something she had a near visceral hatred off. She despised all top-down, government-imposed ideologies, seeing them as being diametrically opposed to human nature in general and freedom of movement and thought in particular. Meanwhile, most of her friends would swing back and forth between being self-declared socialists or communists (though many became disillusioned and even disgusted with the latter), creating a political "norm" that Hurston found herself far removed from. In fact, in Alice Walker's otherwise glowing introduction to Hemenway's 1977 biography, she ended it with a sudden non sequitur denunciation of capitalism, and to her being down with the revolutionary struggle—which to my mind can only be interpreted as a frantic distancing from Hurston's politics, in spite of her love for her art.

Hurston long maintained warm feelings for most of her old Harlem Renaissance cohorts long after that movement had faded and everyone had gone their (physical) separate ways, both as artists and people. But when she herself faced tragedy and hardship in the late '40s, these friends were nowhere to be found, leaving her feeling utterly abandoned and betrayed. This was when (as well as why) she distanced herself from mainstream academic and literary circles and worked in relative creative isolation in her home state of Florida for the last ten years of her life. And while her writing during this time—almost all of which was composed of essays and editorial commentaries—may not have been entirely spiteful, there is an undeniable sense of bitterness in it. And she no longer pulled any punches when it came to taking "unpopular" positions on the issues, especially race-related issues.

That brings up one more irony of her life: she began her writing career hell-bent on transcending race. She wanted to, as she would put it, write about people who simply happened to be Black. Not an easy line to hold, however, when almost every editor and critic was constantly demanding that she address "the race problem." Of course, she did address it, but mainly as a background acknowledgment that yes, this is the world we live in. But she didn't want to write propaganda. She didn't want to instruct the reader on what or how to think. She simply wanted to relay her life experiences and observations in an engaging manner. But this was never enough for her noisier contemporaries, and it seemed to wear her down, since she ended her days writing about almost nothing but race.

Conversely, she rarely addressed her experiences and thoughts on being a self-sufficient woman in the pre–Women's Rights era in essays or in interviews. Despite the fact that much of her work (and all of her best fiction) has an undeniable feminist slant running through it, she was rarely (if ever?) asked to discuss this aspect of her work. In other words, her race was so much on the forefront of everyone's mind that no one took notice of the fact that she was also a woman!

One other thing to keep in mind when reading this book: her struggle. For example, Hurston biographer Valerie Boyd believes that Hurston was literally the only Black woman in the country who was even attempting to make a living as a writer during the depths of the Depression (I assume Boyd wasn't including reporters, copywriters, or other writers for hire in her classification), since by that time the mere handful of Hurston's female peers had gotten married and/or taken on teaching jobs. Keep in mind that Hurston wasn't writing genre fiction either. Her own fiction didn't even belong to a category. Talk about a hard sell! That she made a living at all as a writer is nothing short of miraculous.

Before I sound like I'm advocating a little too strenuously in Ms. Hurston's favor, I feel obliged to mention that, like all humans, she was far from perfect, and her numerous character flaws are on full display in the following pages. As with her own stories, this book is "warts-and-all." Still, none of Hurston's flaws were egregious, let alone malicious, and the only person who truly suffered from them was herself. They also pale in comparison to her incredible generosity (in every sense of the word), as well as her joy for living that even her harshest critics found infectious when in her presence.

Another note: Hurston was renowned for her extreme—some might even argue outrageous—sense of style. She would be seen wearing, say, a Seminole Indian costume one day, and a men's three-piece suit the next, with no explanation given for either. As a cartoonist, I could have had a field day drawing these wild, disparate outfits, but that would have only distracted from the story, so I regretfully felt it necessary to tone down her wardrobe in most instances.

Finally, I'd like to apologize in advance to all the Zora fans out there who I can't help but think will balk at my putting Hurston's own words into a comic book blender just to make this story work as a comic. But brilliant passages simply don't always fit within the cozy confines of a word balloon, sadly. I also didn't want to try to mimic her inimitable way of writing and speaking (no one can imitate her, let alone some pasty-faced twenty-first century Northerner like myself), and the unfortunate result is that her own dialogue is generally much drier than it was in real life. Still, I think I plagiarized her often enough to keep everyone happy. "I'll shoot you nicely and you'll die politely": I had to squeeze that line in somehow!

FIRE!!
THE ZORA NEALE HURSTON STORY

EATONVILLE, FLORIDA, LATE 1890S...

OH, CHARLES, LOOK AT THAT **LITTLE PICKANINNY** GREETING US UP AHEAD!

ISN'T SHE **ADORABLE**?

**HOWDY, FOLKS!**

WHERE Y'ALL **HEADED**?

BUT WE'RE GOING TO THE OCEAN, PA!
MAYBE THEY IS, BUT YOU AIN'T!
WE WERE JUST HAVING FUN WITH HER, IS ALL!
THAT'S QUITE A PRECOCIOUS YOUNGSTER YOU HAVE THERE!

'DEED SHE IS...
TOO BAD FOR ME.
SO LONG, FOLKS!
SWING BY ANY OL' TIME!

SWAT
YEOW!
WHAT WAS THAT FOR?!
F'R TALKIN' TO STRANGERS...
'SPECIALLY WHITE ONES!

BUT DEY SEEMED NICE, PA!
SHO' DEY'S NICE...
TILL DEY AIN'T!

YOU DON'T KNOW WHITE FOLKS LIKE AH DO...
GROWIN' UP IN AN ALL-COLORED TOWN'S MADE YOU UNAWARE OF CERTAIN HARD COLD FACTS.
BUT DEY WAS GOIN' TO DA OCEAN....
I WANNA GO PLACES TOO!

WIT' DAT MOUTH O' YOURS YOU'D BEST STAY PUT..
OTHERWISE YOU'S A LYNCHIN' WAITIN' TA HAPPEN!
WHAT'S A "LYNCHING"?

A "LYING SESSION" OUTSIDE JOE CLARKE'S STORE...

LATER, AT THE HURSTON RESIDENCE...

THOUGH I NEVER UNDERSTOOD WHY YOU MARRIED THAT HIGH YALLER BASTARD IN DEY FIRST PLACE...
=SIGH=
I THOUGHT WE WERE PAST THIS, MAMA.
KING JAMES BIBLE
BIBLE

YOU COME FROM A GOOD FAMILY...
WE OWNED OUR OWN FARM...
YET DEN YOU RUN OFF WIT' SOME COTTON-PICKER FROM OVAH DA CREEK...
JOHN HAD AMBITION...
AND HE'S DONE QUITE WELL FOR HIMSELF...

HE STARTED HIS OWN BUSINESS...
BIG WOOP.
AND HE'S SERVED AS MAYOR...
LIKE HE'D EVER LET YOU FORGET IT.

AND HE'S THE MOST SOUGHT AFTER PREACHER IN THREE COUNTIES—
OH, YOU GOT DAT RIGHT...
SOUGHT AFTER BY DE WOMEN, DAT IS!

MAMA, DON'T YOU START—
OPEN YO' EYES, GIRL!
AN' DON'T TELL ME HE AIN'T BEEN SAMPLIN' DEY WARES, EITHER!
♫

?!?
WHAT KIND O' BOOK IS DAT YOU GOT THERE, CHILD?
IT'S ABOUT THE NORSE GODS, GRANDMA!
A GUEST SPEAKER AT ZORA'S SCHOOL GAVE IT TO HER...
IT'S HER FAVORITE BOOK.

I WANNA BE JUST LIKE ODIN WHEN I GROW UP...
HE DA MAN!
?!? WHO IN BLAZES IS "ODIN"?

SEPT. 18th, 1904...
ZORA, I WANT YOU TO DO A FAVOR FOR ME BEFORE I DIE...
YOU AIN'T DYIN', MAMA.

STILL, IF I DO START TO GO, PLEASE PROMISE ME YOU WON'T LET ANYONE REMOVE THE PILLOW FROM UNDER MY HEAD...
OR COVER THE CLOCK OR MIRROR...
?
WHY WOULD ANYONE DO THAT?

IT'S A CUSTOM 'MONGST OUR PEOPLE...
SILLY SUPERSTITIONS, IF YOU ASK ME...
YOUR PA WILL ALSO TRY TO TURN MY BED SO'S MY FEET WILL BE FACING EAST...
WHY?

IT'S A BAPTIST TRADITION...
AND HIM BEIN' A MINISTER, HE'LL FEEL OBLIGED TO DO SO...
EVEN THOUGH I ASKED HIM NOT TO.
WOULD I HAVE TO FIGHT WITH PA OVER THIS?

JUST REMIND HIM OF MY WISHES, IS ALL...
IN CASE HE FORGETS.
AIN'T GONNA HAPPEN, MA, 'CUZ YOU AIN'T DYIN'!
BESIDES, I'LL BE ALL ALONE IF YOU GO!

DON'T BE SILLY...
YOU'LL STILL HAVE YOUR PA, AND YOUR BROTHERS AND SISTER...
YOU'LL BE FINE.
Y-YES, MAMA.
BUT NO ONE IN THIS WORLD UNDERSTANDS ME EXCEPT FOR YOU!

THAT EVENING...

ALL NIGHT LONG...
THE POOR DEAR...
SHE SUFFERED **SO MUCH**...
I WONDER WHAT'S **REALLY** GOING ON IN PA'S MIND RIGHT NOW.

MOVE TO **JACKSONVILLE** WITH ME, ZORA...
YOU CAN ENROLL IN MY **SCHOOL**...
BUT BOB, WHAT ABOUT **PA**?
YOU DON'T WANT TO BE STUCK HERE WITH **HIM**...
AND HE'S SURE TO **RE-MARRY** ANYWAY.

SOON...
I'M A **NOBODY** IN THIS TOWN...
JUST ANOTHER **COLORED GIRL**.
JACKSONVILLE
FLORIDA
PORTER
TICKETS

AT THE FLORIDA BAPTIST ACADEMY...
YOUR GOOD GRADES DO NOT EXCUSE YOUR **SASSY MOUTH**, MISS HURSTON...
AND PLEASE, DO SOMETHING ABOUT THAT **RAT NEST HAIR** OF YOURS!
GIGGLE

SISTER SARAH ARRIVES...
PA'S RE-MARRIED **ALREADY**?
TO SOME **HORRID TWENTY-YEAR OLD**, NO LESS!
I HAD TO GET **OUT OF THERE**, ZORA...
AND I TOOK **LI'L EVERETT** HERE WITH ME...
HE WON'T BE RAISED BY THAT **WITCH**!

THEN...
YOUR FATHER'S STOPPED PAYING FOR YOUR **ROOM AND BOARD**...
BUT YOU CAN FINISH OUT THE YEAR IF YOU AGREE TO **SCRUB THE FLOORS**...
AFTER THAT... WELL, I **JUST DON'T KNOW**...

ONE YEAR LATER...
MY WIFE IS SICKLY, SO WE NEED FULL-TIME HELP...
THE JOB COMES WITH FREE ROOM AND BOARD...
THAT SOUNDS FINE, SIR.
AT LEAST SOMEONE'S WILLING TO HIRE ME!

SOON...
GOOD MORNING, ZORA...
MY, YOU LOOK FINE TODAY!
UH-OH. HE'S GETTING A LITTLE TOO FRIENDLY...

STAY OUT OF MY ROOM!
AH'M GONNA TELL YO' WIFE!
GO AHEAD! SEE IF I CARE!
I MUST HAVE YOU, ZORA!

I'M GLAD YOU TOLD ME, ZORA...
BUT WHAT CAN I DO?
HE SIMPLY DOESN'T WANT ME ANYMORE! =SOB!=
=SIGH=... NOW WHAT?

I'M GLAD YOU TOLD HER!
NOW WE CAN BE TOGETHER!
RUN AWAY TO CANADA WITH ME!
CANADA?
ARE YOU MAD?
I QUIT!

WEEKS LATER...
DID Y'ALL HEAR ABOUT YOUNG MABEL?
SHE DONE RUN OFF TO CANADA WIT' DAT MARRIED WHITE MAN, MR. JOHNSON!
LORD HAVE MERCY...
SEEMS LAHK DE WHOLE WORLD'S DONE GONE CRAZY!
?!?
THAT'S MY OLD BOSS!

THE WORLD IS CRAZY...
I WANNA GO HOME!
=SIGH=

BACK IN EATONVILLE...
NOW THAT YO' LIVIN' HERE AGAIN, WE NEED TO 'STABLISH A FEW GROUND RULES...
OH?
SUCH AS?

SUCH AS I AM THE MISTRESS OF THIS HOUSE!
YO' MAMA DIED YEARS AGO...
YOU NEED TO ACCEPT DAT FACT AND MOVE ON!
HMPF. LIKE I HAVE A CHOICE...

AND NO MO' CRYIN' 'BOUT HOW YO' MAMA BEQUEATHED HER BED TO YOU...
IT'S MY BED NOW. GOT IT?
GRUMBLE...

AND NO WALKIN' AWAY WHILST AH'M TALKIN' TO YOU!
FLING!
THUNK!
?!?

NEXT TIME I WON'T MISS!
OH, THERE AIN'T GONNA BE A NEXT TIME...

SHOVE
?!?

UMPF...
I'LL SCRATCH YO' EYES OUT...
YOU BIG UGLY HEIFER!
WHO YOU CALLIN' UGLY?

BASH

=GASP= ZORA! MATTIE! WHAT IN BLAZES—
BAM! BAM!

GET OUT!
WUMP

JOHN! COME QUICK!
ZORA'S DONE LOST HER MIND!
?

ZORA, STOP!
YOU'RE GONNA KILL HER!
THAT'S THE IDEA!
BAM! BAM! BAM!

GET OFF OF HER NOW!
NO! LET GO!

I DON'T KNOW WHAT BROUGHT THIS ON...
ALL I KNOW IS YOU CAN'T STAY HERE NO MORE!
FINE! WHO'D WANT TO STAY HERE?

AND SO...
GOOD LORD...
WHAT HAVE I DONE?

ON HER OWN AGAIN...
?!?
SOMEBODY THREW OUT A BOOK!

"PARADISE LOST"...
NEVER HEARD OF IT...
BUT I MIGHT AS WELL GIVE IT A TRY...
PARADISE LOST
By JOHN MILTON

LATER...
THIS BOOK IS GOOD!
THE WRITING IS SO PRETTY...
I WISH I COULD WRITE LIKE THIS....

I ALSO WISH I UNDERSTOOD ALL OF IT...
I DON'T KNOW WHAT A LOT OF THESE WORDS MEAN...
I WISH SOME-ONE COULD TEACH THEM TO ME...
PARADISE LOST

DOGGONIT! I WANT AN EDUCATION SO BAD!
I FEEL SO USELESS WITHOUT ONE!
I DON'T FEEL LIKE MYSELF WITHOUT ONE!
PARADISE LOST

MY BROTHER BOB SAID I COULD JOIN HIM AND HIS WIFE IN NASHVILLE IF I WANT TO...
MAYBE I COULD GO BACK TO SCHOOL THERE...
AT LEAST IT'S WORTH A SHOT.

NASHVILLE, TN, 1912...
I CAN'T AFFORD TO ENROLL YOU IN SCHOOL JUST YET, ZORA...
I'M NOT DONE WITH MED SCHOOL MYSELF...
AND MY WIFE NEEDS HELP WITH OUR NEWBORN...
=SIGH=

MEMPHIS, TN, 1913...
MY NEW PRACTICE IS GOING WELL, I ADMIT...
BUT NOW I'M BUSIER THAN EVER, AND I ALSO HAVE THREE CHILDREN TO FEED, SO—
YOU PROMISED, BOB! NO BACKING OUT!
F P
T O Z
L P E D

LISTEN ZORA, YOU'RE PART OF MY HOUSEHOLD NOW...
AND AS SUCH YOU'LL ALWAYS BE TAKEN CARE OF...
I'M YOUR MAID IS WHAT I AM! AN UNPAID ONE AT THAT!
AND YOU'RE NOT MY FATHER!

BACK IN JACKSONVILLE, 1914...
WE'LL RE-ENROLL YOU IN THE BAPTIST ACADEMY RIGHT AWAY, ZORA...
YOU'LL EARN THAT DIPLOMA IN NO TIME!
THANK YOU, JOHN. I APPRECIATE IT.

ALL I ASK IS THAT YOU REGULARLY ATTEND SUNDAY SERVICES WITH US...
AND HERE, SIGN YOUR NAME IN THE REGISTRY...
WILL DO.
Welcome

THEN...
JOHN, WHERE'S ZORA?
I HAVEN'T SEEN HER ALL DAY...
SHE'S NOT IN HER ROOM...
AND HER BELONGINGS ARE GONE!

I WAS SEVEN WHEN **THE VISIONS** BEGAN. THERE WERE TWELVE IN ALL, AND EACH ONE WOULD FLASH BEFORE ME LONG ENOUGH FOR ME TO STUDY IN **EVERY DETAIL**...
I KNEW THEY WERE A PREVIEW OF THINGS TO COME. MY **INESCAPABLE FATE**.

THUS I KNEW AHEAD OF TIME THAT THE COMFORTING CIRCLE OF MY FAMILY WOULD BE **BROKEN**...
THAT I WOULD WANDER **COLD** AND **FRIENDLESS** FOR A TIME.

I KNEW THAT A SHOTGUN BUILT HOUSE IN NEED OF WHITE PAINT HELD **TORTURE** FOR ME, BUT THAT I MUST **GO**...

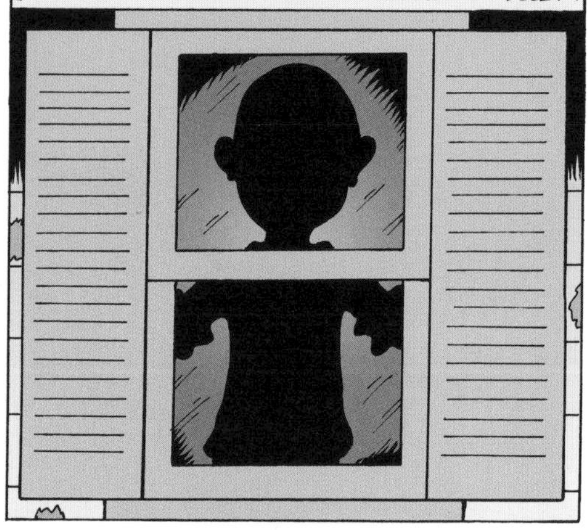
I SAW DEEP LOVE BETRAYED, BUT I HAD TO **KNOW** IT AND **FEEL** IT.

THE LAST VISION WAS OF **TWO FACELESS WOMEN**, ONE YOUNG, ONE OLD, BOTH WAITING FOR ME.
THEY WERE ARRANGING **QUEER SHAPED FLOWERS**, THE LIKES OF WHICH I'D NEVER SEEN BEFORE.

THIS MOMENT WOULD NOT BE THE END OF MY LIFE, BUT A **NEW BEGINNING**...
IT ALSO WOULD MARK THE END OF MY **PILGRIMAGE**.

1916...
WE FOUND A NEW GIRL FOR YOU, MISS M...
SHE COMES HIGHLY RECOMMENDED...
OH, I DON'T WANT HER RESUMÉ...

JUST TELL ME ONE THING, MISS...
ZORA.
MISS ZORA, ARE YOU ENGAGED?
NO, I'M NOT ENGAGED.
GOOD, SINCE MY LAST GIRL RAN OFF ON ME TO GET MARRIED!

HOW DOES $10 A WEEK SOUND?
PLUS FREE ROOM AND BOARD, OF COURSE.
THAT SOUNDS FIVE TIMES BETTER THAN MY LAST JOB!
FINE. YOU'RE HIRED.
UNDO ME, PLEASE.

ON THE ROAD...
STEP ASIDE, FELLOW THESPIANS...
A LOVELY BLONDE AND BRUNETTE ARE COMING THROUGH!
MORE LIKE A "BURNT-NETTE" IF YOU ASK ME, YUCK YUCK!

HUMPF!
WHAT, NO COME-BACK?
NOT EVEN A BIT O' SASS?
NUDGE NUDGE

OH, I'LL GIVE YOU SASS, YOU MULE-HEADED, WALL-EYED, GATOR-FACED, GOAT-BELLIED CAMEL-BACKED, KNOCK-KNEED, FLAT-FOOTED SO'N'SO!

HA HA HA HA HA
OOPS...
DID THAT COME OUT OF ME?

I'M SO GLAD I PAID FOR YOU TO TAKE **MANICURE LESSONS**...
AND NOW YOU AT LEAST HAVE ANOTHER **CAREER OPTION.**
TRUE, THOUGH I'D LIKE TO GO TO **COLLEGE** EVENTUALLY.

OH? TO STUDY **WHAT?**
I'M NOT **SURE**...
AND I STILL HAVE TO FINISH **HIGH SCHOOL** FIRST!
=SIGH=
HERE, LET ME DO **YOUR** NAILS NOW...

I THOUGHT YOU WANTED TO STAY IN THE **THEATER**...
OH, I **LOVE** THE THEATER!
PROBLEM IS, I WANT TO SEE AND DO **EVERYTHING**...
MY HEAD IS **EXPLODING**!

WELL, I HOPE YOU'VE BEEN SAVING YOUR **MONEY**...
AND THAT I'M **PAYING** YOU ENOUGH...
AND NOT WORKING YOU **TOO** HARD.
DOES **THIS** LOOK LIKE "**WORK**"?
THIS IS A **GOOD SHADE** FOR YOU, I THINK.

18 MONTHS LATER...
IT TURNS OUT IT'S **YOU** ABANDONING **ME** FOR WEDDED BLISS, MISS M!
I'LL CERTAINLY MISS THE **THEATER**...
AND **YOU** EVEN MORE, ZORA!
BALTIMORE
TICKETS
PORTER
HAVE YOU MADE YOUR **OWN PLANS** YET?

I LOOKED INTO ENROLLING IN HIGH SCHOOL **HERE**, BUT YOU HAVE TO BE **UNDER 18**...
AND I'M **26**!
SO? JUST TELL 'EM YOU'RE ONLY **SWEET SIXTEEN**...
TRUST ME, YOU **LOOK** IT!

"NICKELING AND DIMERING" IN BALTIMORE, MD, 1917 - '18...

AT NIGHT SCHOOL...

AT MORGAN PREP...

SOON...

A VISIT FROM SISTER SARAH...

HOWARD UNIVERSITY, WASHINGTON, DC, 1921...
I SEE YOU'RE DOING WELL IN ENGLISH AND LATIN...
BUT YOUR MATH AND GREEK SCORES ARE WANTING...
I'VE NEVER GOTTEN ALONG WITH ALGEBRA, SIR...
AND AS FOR GREEK, WELL, 'NUFF SAID...
THIS ISN'T A JOKE!
THIS IS HOWARD, THE FINEST NEGRO UNIVERSITY IN THE WORLD!
SHOW SOME PRIDE, STUDENT! AND SOME GRATITUDE!
HARVARD
Y-YES, SIR! I'M SORRY!
STILL, YOUR FICTION PIECES ARE QUITE IMPRESSIVE...
WHY, THANK YOU, PROFESSOR!
THE STYLUS Magazine Howard U.
ONLY I SEE YOU JUMP FROM A PROPER ENGLISH NARRATION TO DIALOG USING AN EXAGGERATED SOUTHERN NEGRO DIALECT...
IT'S HARDLY EXAGGERATED, SIR...
THAT'S HOW FOLKS TALK IN MY HOMETOWN.
OH? WELL, I SUGGEST YOU STICK WITH THE FORMER...
UNLESS YOU CAN MAKE THE LATTER SOUND LESS LIKE PANDERING...
Y-YES, SIR...
JOHN REDDING GOES TO SEA By ZORA N. HURSTON
"PANDERING" TO WHOM?
LATER...
WOW, ZORA! DR. LOCKE ACTUALLY TALKED TO YOU!
I THOUGHT HE ONLY "LIKED" BOYS, IF YOU GET MY DRIFT!
HE WAS HARDLY FLIRTING...
JUST MAKING ME FEEL LIKE A FRAUD, AS USUAL.
DR. ALAIN LOCKE P.H.D.
HOW TYPICAL. THAT WOMAN-HATER!
OH, I LIKE WHEN HE CRITICIZES MY WORK...
IT MAKES ME THAT MUCH MORE DETERMINED TO PROVE HIM WRONG!

RUSH WEEK...
THOSE GIRLS ARE IN THE ALPHA SORORITY...
THEY WEAR THE FANCIEST CLOTHES...
UGH. SOUNDS EXPENSIVE.
THEN THERE'S THE DELTAS...
THEY HAVE THE LIGHTEST SKIN...
MY, QUITE AN ACCOMPLISHMENT.
AND THEN THERE'S THE ZETAS...
THEY'RE THE SMARTEST GIRLS.
GOOD. I'M PLEDGING WITH THEM.
WELCOME

—SAY, WHO'S THE HANDSOME STUD ON THE PIANO?
GET IN LINE, GIRL! THAT'S HERBERT SHEEN...

HE'S PRE-MED, I DO BELIEVE.
A FUTURE DOCTOR AND A MUSICIAN? I LIKE THAT COMBO!
...MY SWEET JELLYROLL...

(UH-OH! LOOKS LIKE HE'S GOT HIS EYE ON YOU, TOO!)
CARE FOR A GAME OF POOL, MISS?

SOON...
WE HAVE A LOT IN COMMON, ZORA...
OUR FATHERS WERE BOTH PREACHERS...
ONLY YOURS WAS A METHODIST.
OURS WOULD BE A MIXED MARRIAGE! HA HA!

WHO SAID ANYTHING ABOUT MARRIAGE?
THAT IS WHERE YOU WERE GOING WITH THIS, WEREN'T YOU?
EITHER WAY, I'M NOT READY.

YES, I SUPPOSE WE SHOULD AT LEAST WAIT UNTIL AFTER GRADUATION...
OR EVEN LONGER...
WHY SPOIL THE FUN? TEE-HEE!

LATE 1924...

LATER...

SOON, AT THE HOME OF "OPPORTUNITY"'S EDITOR CHARLES S. JOHNSON...

MAY 1: AT THE AFTER-PARTY FOR OPPORTUNITY MAGAZINE'S LITERARY AWARDS CEREMONY...
WHAT A HUGE TURNOUT WE HAVE THIS EVENING!
INDEED, THIS FEELS LIKE THE START OF A MOVEMENT!
HOW ABOUT THAT LIVELY YOUNG WOMAN WHO WON ALL THOSE 2nd PLACE PRIZES!
YES! ONLY WHAT WAS HER NAME AGAIN?
IT'S ZORA! AUTHOR OF THE PLAY...
"COLOR STRUCK"!
WHOA! I'M COLOR STRUCK BY THAT SCARF!
ZORA! OVER HERE!
THERE'S SEVERAL PEOPLE I WANT YOU TO MEET...
WHAT A SHOW OFF!
THIS IS THE BEST-SELLING AUTHOR FANNIE HURST...
AND NEW YORK TIMES MUSIC CRITIC CARL VAN VECHTEN...
WE LOVE YOUR WORK, ZORA...
AND YOUR SENSE OF STYLE...
LET'S BE BEST FRIENDS!
AND THIS IS ANNIE NATHAN MEYER, FOUNDER OF BARNARD COLLEGE...
I'M TOLD YOU HAVEN'T FINISHED YOUR STUDIES AT HOWARD, MRS. HURSTON.
ER, NO, I HAVEN'T. YOU SEE, I—
WOULD YOU CONSIDER TRANSFERRING TO BARNARD?
IT'S ABOUT TIME WE HAD OUR FIRST NEGRO STUDENT!
SERIOUSLY?!
MY CUP RUNNETH OVER TONIGHT!

THAT FALL...
SO FAR THIS SCHOOL SEEMS EASIER THAN HOWARD...
AND NOW I CAN COMPLETE MY STUDIES RIGHT HERE IN NEW YORK CITY...
BARNARD COLLEGE OF COLUMBIA UNIVERSITY
(WHERE DOES SHE THINK SHE'S GOING?)
(THE SERVICE ENTRANCE IS THAT WAY, HON'! HA HA!)

STILL, THIS SCHOOL IS EXPENSIVE...
WE EVEN HAVE TO PAY FOR OUR OWN GOLF OUTFITS!
AM I THE ONLY ONE HERE NOT MADE OF MONEY?
FRENCH
FRENCH
FRENCH
(IS THAT A FRENCH TEXTBOOK SHE'S HOLDING?)
(I HOPE SHE ISN'T IN OUR FRENCH CLASS!)

=GASP!= (SHE IS IN OUR CLASS!)
(IS BARNARD ACCEPTING ANYONE THESE DAYS?)
PLEASE TAKE YOUR SEATS, LADIES...
Bonjour, Etudiants

THE HOURS AT THIS PLACE ARE INSANE AS WELL...
HOW CAN I POSSIBLY FIND A JOB THAT WILL—
OH, AND MISS HURSTON — I JUST RECIEVED GOOD NEWS FROM THE TRUSTEES' OFFICE...
SCHEDULE

THE ESTEEMED AUTHOR FANNIE HURST HAS OFFERED YOU A JOB AS HER PERSONAL SECRETARY...
CONGRATULATIONS!
FANNIE HURST ?!?
?!?

AFTER CLASS...
OOH! ZORA! OUR SORORITY IS HOSTING A MIXER TOMORROW...
WON'T YOU PLEASE COME?
YOU CAN BRING A DATE!

LATER, AT FANNIE HURST'S 5th AVENUE APARTMENT...

ZORA! I WAS HOPING YOU'D BE HERE!
HELLO AGAIN, MR. VAN VECHTEN!

PLEASE, CALL ME CARLO...
ALL MY FRIENDS DO!
?!? YOU'RE WEARING A LADY STYLE WATCH.

OH! YES, THOUGH THEY'RE MARKETING WRISTWATCHES TO MEN NOW...
I PREDICT MOST MEN WILL BE WEARING THEM SOON...
I JUST LOVE TO START TRENDS!
CARLO! SO GOOD TO SEE YOU!

FANNIE! I MUST TELL YOU ALL ABOUT THIS NEW HARLEM NIGHTCLUB I JUST DISCOVERED!
REALLY, CARLO, MUST YOU START GOING ON ABOUT HARLEM AS SOON AS YOU ARRIVE?

BUT FANNIE, I—
IN FACT, I'M DECLARING THIS A "TABOO TEA"...
WHEREIN I, THE HOSTESS, CHOOSE ONE SUBJECT THAT IS STRICTLY OFF LIMITS.

OH, AND WHAT SUBJECT WOULD THAT BE?
"THE NEGRO."
HAW!

HARLEM, 1926...
I REALLY APPRECIATE YOU ESCORTING ME UPTOWN TONIGHT, ZORA...
I'VE BEEN PERSONA NON GRATA UP HERE EVER SINCE MY NEW NOVEL CAME OUT.
YES, WELL, I'M NOT SURPRISED...
NEWSTAND
W. 135th ST
8th Ave.
UPTOWN IRT 2,3

I MEAN, WHAT WERE YOU THINKING, NAMING THAT BOOK "NIGGER HEAVEN"?
IT'S A METAPHOR, ZORA!

I KNOW! AND IT'S ALSO BESIDE THE POINT—
WHOA! WHERE DO YOU THINK YOU'RE GOING?
SMALLS PARADISE

DON'T ACT LIKE YOU DON'T KNOW US, CHARLIE.
YOU'RE WELCOME HERE ANY TIME, ZORA...
BUT THAT DINGE QUEEN YOU'RE WITH HAS GOT TO GO.

WATCH YOUR TONGUE!
CARLO HAS DONE MORE TO PROMOTE YOUR CLUB THAN ANYONE...
AND LOOK! THE PLACE IS PACKED!
OH, SURE: PACKED WITH WHITE THRILL-SEEKERS WHO USE CARLO'S NEW BOOK AS A PERVERT TOURIST'S GUIDE!

YES, SHAME ON CARLO FOR FAILING TO PORTRAY US HARLEMITES AS THE CLEAN-LIVING, MIDDLE-CLASS CHURCH-GOERS THAT WE ALL REALLY ARE...

AND I NOTICE YOU'VE YET TO TURN ANY OF THESE NEW FOLKS AWAY...
S'MATTER? THEIR MONEY MAKIN' YOU LAZY?
=SIGH= I GIVE UP...
TAKE A SEAT, CARLO.
YAY!

AND SO...
THANKS, ZORA!
I'M SO HAPPY NOW!
WELL I'M NOT...
IF THERE'S ONE THING I DESPISE, IT'S SELECTIVE OUTRAGE!

AT ZORA AND BRUCE NUGENT'S PLACE...

A RENT PARTY! HOSTED BY ZORA, BRUCE, AND THEIR NEW ROOMMATE WALLACE THURMAN...

MAN, I AM FED UP WITH W.E.B. DU BOIS AND THIS SELF-RIGHTEOUS RAG OF HIS!
HE THINKS ALL BLACK ARTISTS SHOULD ONLY CREATE PROPAGANDA...
HE SAID SO HIMSELF!
THE CRISIS
"DR. DUBIOUS," THAT'S WHAT I CALL HIM!

HE ASSUMES WE ALL HAVE THE SAME AGENDA...
HIS AGENDA!
SAME GOES FOR THIS THING, WHICH IS JUST A MOUTHPIECE FOR THE SOCIALIST PARTY!
WHILE THIS ONE HAS BECOME HOPELESSLY BOURGEOIS...
The Messenger
OPPORTUNITY
PHOOEY!

YET ALL OF THESE PUBLISHERS ACT LIKE THEY OWN US...
WE'RE A PART OF DU BOIS'S SO-CALLED "TALENTED TENTH"...
WHILE LOCKE CLAIMS WE REPRESENT HIS "NEW NEGRO" MOVEMENT...
GRRR... DON'T GET ME STARTED...

LOCKE'S ALWAYS PARADING US IN FRONT OF RICH WHITE FOLKS...
CLUCKING LIKE A MAMA HEN TO MAKE SURE WE BEHAVE CORRECTLY...
HAW!
OUR SO-CALLED BLACK LEADERS ARE OBSESSED WITH WHAT WHITE PEOPLE THINK...
CLUCK! CLUCK!

WELL I FOR ONE DON'T CARE WHAT ANYONE THINKS!
THAT'S NOT WHY I BECAME A WRITER!
ME, TOO! I—
WAIT— SINCE WHEN ARE YOU A WRITER, BRUCE?

SINCE RIGHT NOW!
I FEEL INSPIRED!
I WANT TO WRITE ABOUT BEING A MALE PROSTITUTE!
AND NO ONE CAN STOP ME!
I FEEL INSPIRED, TOO...

I'M TIRED OF WORRYING ABOUT WHAT THE UPTIGHT, SELF-CONSCIOUS BLACK MIDDLE-CLASS THINK OF US AS WELL...
WE SHOULD ONLY CONCERN OURSELVES WITH THE TRUTH!
AMEN TO THAT!
WE'RE EXPECTED TO ALWAYS PORTRAY OURSELVES AS VICTIMS AND MARTYRS...
BUT BLACK FOLKS AREN'T SAINTS! WE'RE PEOPLE!

I MYSELF WANT TO WRITE ABOUT HOW BIGOTED OUR OWN PEOPLE ARE ABOUT SKIN COLOR...
I SHOULD KNOW, BEING BLACK AS COAL MYSELF!
PROBLEM IS, WHO WOULD PUBLISH SUCH STORIES?

LET'S PUBLISH OUR OWN MAGAZINE!
I MEAN, WHY THE HELL NOT?
YES! LET'S DO IT!
I'M ON FIRE NOW!

BUT WHERE WILL WE GET THE MONEY FROM?
WHO CARES! I JUST HOPE WE GET BANNED IN BOSTON!
BANNED IN BOSTON! BANNED IN BOSTON!
WHAT SHOULD WE CALL THIS MAGAZINE?

LET'S CALL IT "FIRE!!!"
"FIRE!"?
WITH AN EXCLAMATION POINT?
THREE EXCLAMATION POINTS!
HMMM... I DO HAVE A LITTLE MONEY SAVED...

THREE?
THAT'S A BIT EXCESSIVE, DON'T YOU THINK?
FINE, TWO, THEN...
CALL IT A COMPROMISE...
ALL I KNOW IS ONE ISN'T ENOUGH!

ONE YEAR LATER...
SAY WHAT?!
ALL THE REMAINING COPIES OF "FIRE!!" WERE DESTROYED IN A FIRE...
PRETTY PROPHETIC, HUH?

THERE WERE OTHER PYRRHIC OMENS AS WELL...
REMEMBER WHEN YOUR KID BROTHER USED MY STORY FOR KINDLING WHEN HE WAS STAYING HERE?
I WANTED TO KILL HIM FOR THAT!
SO YOU HAD TO WRITE A SECOND DRAFT. BIG DEAL...
HE DID YOU A FAVOR, IF YOU ASK ME.

I MAINLY FEEL SORRY FOR WALLACE...
HE PAID FOR MOST OF THE PRINT COSTS...
HE'LL NEVER MAKE HIS MONEY BACK NOW!
AND IT NEVER GOT BANNED IN BOSTON.

IT NEVER MADE IT TO BOSTON!
WE NEVER FOUND A DISTRIBUTOR!
IT MADE IT TO BALTIMORE, SADLY...
WHERE THIS REVIEWER CALLED MY STORY "EFFEMINATE TOMMYROT"...
BALTIMORE AFRO-AMERICAN
WHAT SELF-RESPECTING BLACK MAN USES A WORD LIKE "TOMMYROT"?!

AND DU BOIS REACTED TO IT LIKE IT WAS A SLAP IN THE FACE...
WHICH I GUESS IT WAS...

OH, BRUCE! WHAT WERE WE THINKING?!?
AWW, ZORA, DON'T...
COME GET YO' SUGAR...

SOMETIMES I FEEL DOOMED TO BE FOREVER MISUNDERSTOOD.
YOU 'N' ME BOTH, BABY...
YOU 'N' ME BOTH.

MEANWHILE, BACK AT SCHOOL...
"ANTHROPOLOGY 101, WITH PROFESSOR FRANZ BOAS"...
THAT'S AN EXCELLENT COURSE!
ARE YOU THINKING OF TAKING IT, ZORA?

IT DOES LOOK INTERESTING..
AND I JUST NEED A FEW MORE ELECTIVES TO GET MY DEGREE,
OH, YOU'LL LOVE IT, AS WELL AS "PAPA FRANZ"...
ONLY DON'T LET HIM HEAR YOU CALL HIM THAT!

AND SO...
CULTURE IS ESSENTIAL TO HUMAN SURVIVAL...
FOR IT IS ROOTED IN MAN'S RELATIONSHIP WITH HIS ENVIRONMENT...
AND SERVES AS A TEACHING TOOL FOR FUTURE GENERATIONS...
PROF. FRANZ BOAS
WHILE ALSO GIVING THE COMMUNITY A SHARED SENSE OF IDENTITY...

VARIED ENVIRONMENTS RESULT IN DRASTICALLY DIFFERENT CULTURES...
WHICH, WHEN THEY COME INTO CONTACT, CAN LEAD TO DISRUPTIONS...
WHICH IN TURN CREATES NEW, HYBRID CULTURES...
AMERICA BEING A SUPREME EXAMPLE...

BUT WHAT MOST FASCINATES ANTHROPOLOGISTS ARE THE MORE ISOLATED COMMUNITIES...
ONES WHOSE CULTURES REMAIN IN A RELATIVELY UNADULTERATED STATE...
THAT SOUNDS LIKE MY HOMETOWN!

SUCH COMMUNITIES ARE TO BE TREASURED, SINCE THEY ARE ALL DOOMED TO EXTINCTION...
AND BY STUDYING THEM NOW, THEY SERVE AS DOCUMENTATION OF OUR FUTURE'S PAST.
I NEED TO GO BACK HOME AGAIN...
I WANT TO PUT EATONVILLE UNDER A MICROSCOPE!

LATER, IN PROF. BOAS'S OFFICE...
WESTERN SCIENTISTS HAVE LONG CLAIMED THAT DARK-SKINNED PEOPLE HAVE SMALLER SKULLS...
DO THEY NOW.

THE IMPLICATION BEING THAT THEY HAVE SMALLER BRAINS...
AND THUS ARE LESS INTELLIGENT.
HMPF. WHAT HOOEY!

INDEED, AND I INTEND TO PROVE IT'S HOOEY BY MEASURING A WIDE SAMPLING OF NEGROID SKULLS.
I SEE...

SO YOU WANT ME TO WALK AROUND HARLEM WITH THIS CALIPER GOING "YOU THERE! LET ME MEASURE YO' HAID!"
YES. IN SO MANY WORDS...

I'D DO IT MYSELF, ONLY I FEAR I'LL BE ASSAULTED...
WHEREAS YOU POSESS A MOST DISARMING PERSONALITY...
SAY NO MORE...
I'LL DO IT!
SOUNDS LIKE FUN!

MEANWHILE, WE'VE ASSEMBLED ENOUGH FUNDING FOR YOUR FIELD STUDY PROPOSAL...
SO IT LOOKS LIKE YOU'LL BE HEADING BACK TO FLORIDA SOON!
REALLY?

OH, THANK YOU, PAPA FRANZ!
?!? "PAPA FRANZ"?

WHAT DID YOU JUST CALL THE PROFESSOR, YOUNG LADY?
OOPS! I'M SORRY!
OH, IT'S FINE...

YOU SEE, I AM ZORA'S PAPA...
JUST ONE OF MY PAST MISSTEPS, IS ALL.
HAW!
?!?

FLORIDA, 1927...
EXCUSE ME, GOOD SIRS...
DO YOU HAVE ANY LOCAL LORE YOU'D LIKE TO SHARE?
SAY WHAT NOW?
WHO THE HELL ARE YOU?
FISH FRY

MY RESEARCH GRANT IS ALMOST ALL SPENT, AND I'VE HARDLY COLLECTED A THING...
I SPENT WAY TOO MUCH ON MY CAR...
AND MY HAT...
AND MY GUN!
AN ARMED NEGRESS?
PLEASE DON'T SHOOT ME!
NOW I'VE SEEN EVERYTHING!

SOON...
I'M GETTING NOWHERE, PROFESSOR BOAS!
I DON'T KNOW WHAT I'M DOING!
I'VE LET YOU DOWN! =SOB=
CALM DOWN, ZORA!
FRONT DESK
PLEASE LIMIT PHONE USE TO 5 MIN.

FORGET THAT YOU'RE AN ANTHROPOLOGY STUDENT FOR NOW...
JUST BE ZORA FROM EATONVILLE, AND IMMERSE YOURSELF...
YOU CAN PUT YOUR "SCIENTIST" HAT BACK ON LATER...
YES, YES, OF COURSE...
IN FACT, I SHOULD GO BACK TO EATONVILLE...

BACK IN EATONVILLE...
IT SHO' IS GOOD TO SEE YOU AGAIN, ZORA!
IT'S GOOD TO BE BACK!
TELL ME, DO FOLKS STILL GATHER AND SWAP TALL TALES AT JOE CLARK'S STORE?
OF COURSE!
NOTHIN' EVAH CHANGES 'ROUND HERE.

...SO JOHN SAYS "I SAW NO DEER, JUST A MAN WIT' A RACK O' CHAIRS ON HIS HAID"!
THA'S A LIE!
YOU'S FULLA MONKEYS AND MOONSHINE!
I'M GOINTER TELL ONE NOW!
HA HA!
THIS IS WHERE I SHOULD'VE STARTED!
...CHICK MAH CHICK MAH CRANY CROW... ♪

LATER, IN JACKSONVILLE, FL...
MY RESEARCH GRANT ALSO OBLIGES ME TO COMPILE THE NAMES OF EVERY BLACK-OWNED BUSINESS OF THIS COUNTY'S HISTORY...
DUVAL COUNTY RECORDS
BUT THIS IS SO TEDIOUS AND TIME CONSUMING!

AND I ALSO AGREED TO WRITE A NOVELIZATION OF ANNIE NATHAN MEYER'S ANTI-LYNCHING PLAY...
ONLY WHEN WILL I EVER GET THAT DONE?

I'M ALSO TOO LONELY TO CONCENTRATE!
HERBERT SAID HE'S STILL WILLING TO MARRY ME...
MAYBE I SHOULD TAKE HIM UP ON IT...

A FEW WEEKS LATER...
SO THIS IS WHAT MARRIED LIFE IS LIKE, EH?
HMPF...
WHERE'S THE FIREWORKS?!?
ZZZZZ...

AND NOW HE WANTS ME TO MOVE TO CHICAGO WITH HIM...
HE'S STARTED A PRACTICE THERE, SO HE HAS TO GO BACK...
AND HE'D NEVER ADJUST TO MY TRANSIENT LIFESTYLE...

BUT I DON'T WANT TO MOVE TO CHICAGO!
AND I'M ONLY JUST NOW FINDING MY TRUE CALLING...
AM I TO GIVE IT ALL UP JUST LIKE THAT?

THIS WAS A HUGE MISTAKE...
I'LL TRY TO MAKE THIS WORK, BUT IF NOT...
WELL, I JUST HOPE HE'LL FORGIVE ME...
ZZZZZ...

LATER, IN MOBILE, AL...
?!? LANGSTON?
WHAT ARE YOU DOING HERE?
I WAS ABOUT TO ASK YOU THE SAME QUESTION...
AND WHY THE GUN?

DAMN, THIS FOOD IS GOOD...
THESE SOUTHERN NEGROES SURE KNOW HOW TO THROW A PARTY!
DON'T TELL THE DO-GOODERS UP NORTH THAT, THOUGH...
THEY'RE SUPPOSED TO ALL BE DOWNTRODDEN AND MISERABLE DOWN HERE, REMEMBER?

SOON...
THE BLUES IS THE GREATEST ART FORM OUR COUNTRY HAS EVER PRODUCED...
OH, ZORA, BE SERIOUS...
I AM SERIOUS!
...MAMA DON'T 'LLOW NO EASY RIDERS 'ROUND HERE...

I LIKE THE BLUES AS MUCH AS ANYONE, BUT I THINK YOU'RE OVERSTATING YOUR CASE...
I'M NOT...
THE NEGRO FARTHEST DOWN HAS MORE PURE POETRY IN HIM THAN ANY-ONE ELSE I'VE EVER MET...
...I DON'T CARE WHAT MAMA SAY...
IT'S AS DEEP AS THE SOIL.

DRIVING BACK TO NEW YORK IN ZORA'S CAR, "SASSY SUSIE"...
LET ME LEND YOU SOME MONEY, LANGSTON...
DON'T BE SHY...
I CAN TELL YOU NEEDS...
STOP TRYING TO BABY ME, ZORA!

BESIDES, I'M WELL TAKEN CARE OF THESE DAYS...
OH? BY WHOM?
DON'T BOTHER ASKING...

BECAUSE I'VE BEEN SWORN TO SECRECY...
AH-HA! A SECRET BENEFACTOR, EH?
YOU TELL ME WHO IT IS OR I'LL STOMP YOUR GUTS OUT!

LATER, AT AN UPSCALE PARK AVENUE APARTMENT...

MORE FOLKLORE GATHERING, LOUGHMAN, FL, 1928...

THAT EVENING...
HOW ABOUT A DANCE, ZORA?
OR ARE YOU GONNA KEEP 'VOIDIN' ME ALL NIGHT?
=SIGH= VERY WELL...
YOU WORE ME DOWN, SLIM!
...POLK COUNTY BLUES...

UH OH...
I'LL, UH, CATCH YOU LATER, ZORA...
HUH?
BUT WE ONLY JUST STARTED—

PREPARE TO MEET YO' JESUS, YOU JEZEBEL!
=GASP!=
SHE'S GOT ME CORNERED!

RUN, ZORA!
POW!
OOF!

FINISH HER OFF, BIG SWEET!
SHE HAD IT COMIN'!
LOOK OUT FO' THAT KNIFE!
JOOK

=WHEW!=
I THINK I'M DONE WITH THIS LOCALE...
GUESS I'LL POINT MY TOES TOWARD NEW ORLEANS!
VAROOOM

LATER, IN NEW ORLEANS, LA...
I JUST FOUND WHITE DUST ON MY FRONT STEP...
AND BROKEN EGG SHELLS...
DO NOT STEP OVER IT!
THAT'S A BAD HEX!
YOU NEED TO WASH IT AWAY FIRST...
USE LYE...
AND A YOUNG BOY'S URINE.
YES, SUH! THANK YOU, DR. TURNER!
DR. TURNER? I—
?!? YOU AGAIN?
HOW MANY TIMES MUST I SHOO YOU AWAY?
YOU WORKIN' FO' THE POLICE?
WHAT? NO!
I JUST WANT TO—
I TOL' YOU ALREADY, I DON'T NEED NO APPRENTICE...
TRY SOMEONE ELSE.
I ALREADY HAVE STUDIED UNDER TWO OTHER TWO-HEADED DOCTORS...
BUT EVERYONE SAYS YOU'RE THE BEST!
IN FACT, THEY SAY YOU STUDIED UNDER YOUR AUNT, THE GREAT MARIE LAVEAU.
YOU HEARD CORRECT.
SO TELL ME, WHAT WAS SHE LIKE?
WAS SHE AS POWERFUL AS THEY SAY?
OR ARE THEY JUST TALL TALES?
TALL TALES ?!?
ZZZZ
WOMAN, YOU HAVE NO IDEA!
MY AUNT KNEW MORE THAN EVERY OTHER ROOT DOCTOR AND CONJURER PUT TOGETHER...
SHE WAS A LATTER-DAY MOSES!
HERE, I WANNA SHOW YOU SUMPTHIN'...
HISSSSSS
I'M IN!

WEEKS LATER... TO PREPARE FOR MY INITIATION, I DEVOTED NINE DAYS TO **CLEAN LIVING** AND **CLEAN THOUGHTS**...

ANOTHER HOODOO DOCTOR REMOVED MY **NEW UNDERWEAR** AND PLACED IT ON AN ALTAR, WHILE DR. TURNER CROWNED ME AND DRAPED ME IN **SNAKE SKINS**...

TURNER CALLED TO ME, A **TUB OF WATER** BETWEEN US...

I STEPPED INTO THE TUB, THEN OUT OF IT. "I SEE HER CONQUERING WITH **LIGHTNING**, AND MAKING HER ROAD WITH **THUNDER**," HE SAID OF ME.

I LAY DOWN AGAIN, WITH GREAT **CEREMONY**. TURNER PAINTED A LIGHTNING BOLT DOWN MY BACK...

THIS WAS TO BE MY **SIGN**. THE GREAT ONE WILL SPEAK TO ME THROUGH **STORMS**, I WAS TOLD.

LATER, WITH CONJURER JOE WATSON...

PASS EACH BONE THROUGH YOUR LIPS, UNTIL YOU COME TO ONE THAT IS PARTICULARLY BITTER...

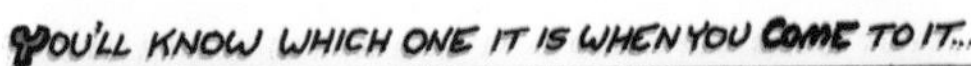

LATER STILL, UNDER THE TUTELAGE OF THE "LOVE DOCTOR" KITTY BROWN...
MAH MAN DONE LEFT ME FO' ANOTHER WOMAN!
AN' HE TOOK ALL MAH SAVINS WIT' HIM!
HE NEEDS TO DIE!
AND DIE HE SHALL...
THOUGH IT'LL COST YOU PLENTY.

WE MUST ARRANGE A DEATH DANCE, ZORA...
ONLY YOU MUST DANCE IN MY PLACE, SINCE I'M GETTING TOO OLD.
YES, MA'AM...
JUST TELL ME WHAT TO DO.

SOON...
SUMMON DEATH WITH FACES AND GESTURES...
OUR TARGET SHOULD BE DEAD WITHIN NINE DAYS...
YES, YES...
BOOM BOOM

FIVE DAYS LATER...
YO, MAN...
WORD HAS IT YOU ONLY HAVE FOUR DAYS TO LIVE!
?!?
WHATCHOO MEAN?

YO' EX PAID A VISIT TO MISS KITTY...
WHO HELD A DEATH DANCE IN YO' HONOR!
OH, GO ON...
I DON'T BUY INTO THAT HOODOO HOKUM NO HOW!

HAVE IT YO' WAY, BROTHUH...
IT WAS NICE KNOWIN' YA! HA HA!
THESE CHEST PAINS OF MINE HAVE BEEN GETTING WORSE LATELY...
COULD IT BE?

AND SO...
MAH MAN CAME BACK TO ME!
PLEASE DON'T LET HIM DIE, MISS KITTY!
I CAN UNDO THE SPELL...
BUT IT'LL COST YOU PLENTY...
WHAT A RACKET!

REUNITED WITH LANGSTON HUGHES, WESTFIELD, NJ, 1930...
"GODMOTHER" SET US UP IN THIS SMALL TOWN SO WE'D BE LESS DISTRACTED.
JUST AS WELL, SINCE THIS LINGERING DEPRESSION MAKES THE CITY TOO DEPRESSING TO WORK IN...
EVERYONE WE KNOW IS OUT OF WORK!

YOU AND I ARE LUCKY TO STILL HAVE GODMOTHER MASON'S PATRONAGE...
EVEN IF SHE IS STARTING TO GET ON MY NERVES...
NO KIDDING! WHAT A TEMPER SHE HAS!
I'M CONSTANTLY PLACATING HER!

AND NOW THAT OLD PROFESSOR LOCKE HAS HER EAR, THEY'RE BOTH MEDDLING IN MY WORK.
THAT WEASEL! HE BUTTERS HER UP JUST SO HE CAN CONTROL WHO DOES OR DOESN'T GET HER SUPPORT!
I CAN'T SAY I RESPECT HIM MUCH ANYMORE...

AND NOW MASON IS CLAIMING OWNERSHIP OF ALL MY RESEARCH!
AS IF SHE CAN OWN THE RIGHTS TO MY OWN LIFE EXPERIENCES!
I CAN'T PUBLISH A THING NOW WITHOUT HER APPROVAL!
CONTRACT ADDENDUM
*SIGH*... YOU AND ME BOTH...

BUT I STILL WANT TO WRITE THIS PLAY WITH YOU, LANGSTON...
IT'LL BE THE FIRST HONEST MUSICAL COMEDY ABOUT SOUTHERN BLACK FOLK!
WELL, NOT BEING FROM THE SOUTH MYSELF, THIS WILL MOSTLY BE YOUR PLAY, ZORA...
MULE BONE
BUT I'LL GLADLY HELP YOU IN ANY WAY I CAN.

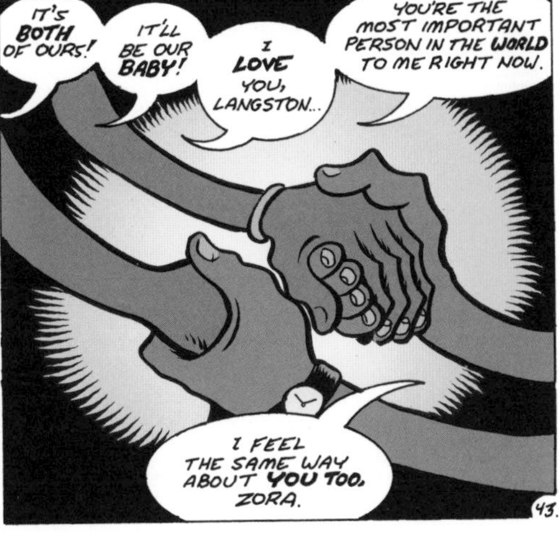
IT'S BOTH OF OURS!
IT'LL BE OUR BABY!
I LOVE YOU, LANGSTON...
YOU'RE THE MOST IMPORTANT PERSON IN THE WORLD TO ME RIGHT NOW.
I FEEL THE SAME WAY ABOUT YOU TOO. ZORA.

SOON...
ZORA, MEET LOUISE THOMPSON...
SHE JUST GOT DIVORCED FROM OUR OLD FRIEND WALLACE THURMAN...
?!? YOU WERE MARRIED TO WALLACE?

NO OFFENSE, HON, BUT THAT BOY'S AS QUEER AS A THREE DOLLAR BILL!
SO I FOUND OUT... THE HARD WAY...
HE'D HOPED I'D BE ABLE TO HELP TO "CURE" HIM.
WELL NOW SHE'S HERE TO HELP US...

...SINCE GODMOTHER HIRED HER TO TAKE DICTATION FOR US!
THAT'S WONDERFUL...
SEEING HOW MUCH I HATE TO TYPE...
SO PLEASE, HAVE A SEAT!

AND SO...
..."THE WOMAN I MARRY AIN'T BORN YET...
..."AND HER MAMA IS ALREADY DEAD"...
HAW! WHAT A GREAT LINE!
ZORA, YOU'RE A SCREAM!

(SAY, ZORA, I THINK WE SHOULD GIVE LOUISE CO-WRITING CREDIT FOR THE PLAY)...
("CREDIT?" FOR WHAT?)
(SHE'S A TYPIST, LANGSTON!)

(OR AT LEAST A SHARE OF THE PROFITS)...
(GODMOTHER IS PAYING HER ALREADY!)
(THIS IS OUR PLAY, AND NOBODY ELSE'S!)

(I JUST WANT TO BE FAIR, IS ALL)...
(PROMISE ME YOU'LL AT LEAST CONSIDER IT.)
I WAS AFRAID THIS MIGHT HAPPEN...
SHE'S COMING BETWEEN US!

CLEVELAND, OH, 1931...
WE'RE SO GLAD YOU AND MISS HURSTON HAVE BOTH AGREED TO LET US PRODUCE YOUR PLAY, LANGSTON.
I'M GLAD TOO, ESPECIALLY AFTER ALL THE ILL WILL THAT DEVELOPED BETWEEN ME AND ZORA...
KARAMU THEATER
WE USED TO BE SO CLOSE, BUT THIS PLAY CREATED QUITE A RIFT BETWEEN US...
NOT TOO MENTION THE LAWSUITS, AND ACCUSATIONS...
ZORA STILL INSISTS SHE WROTE MOST OF THE PLAY HERSELF.

SHE DID! I NEVER DISPUTED THAT!
I ALSO AGREED TO EXCLUDE MISS THOMPSON FROM ALL CREDITS AND PROCEEDS...
MULE BONE (A BONE OF CONTENTION) BY ZORA N. HURSTON AND LANGSTON HUGHES
I JUST WANT TO PUT THIS ALL BEHIND US!

IT'S BEEN A TRYING YEAR FOR ME ALL TOGETHER...
MY HEALTH IS SHOT, AND MRS. MASON HAS ABRUPTLY STOPED SUPPORTING ME...
IN FACT, THIS PLAY IS THE ONLY CURRENT PROJECT OF MINE THAT—
THERE'LL BE NO PLAY!

I JUST FOUND OUT LOUISE THOMPSON IS IN TOWN!
YOU SWORE TO ME SHE WAS OUT OF THE PICTURE!
SHE IS!
SHE'S ONLY IN TOWN TO VISIT RELATIVES!

OH? THEN WHY WAS SHE HERE AT THIS VERY THEATER LAST NIGHT?
THE TWO OF YOU ARE PLOTTING AGAINST ME!
ZORA, I ASSURE YOU, I—

SAVE YOUR BREATH!
THIS IS THE LAST STRAW!
WE'RE THROUGH, LANGSTON!

=SIGH= IT'S JUST AS WELL...
OTHERWISE THAT VEXING WOMAN WOULD SURELY BE THE DEATH OF ME.

LATER, AT GODMOTHER'S "THRONE"...

THEN, AT VAN VECHTEN'S STUDIO...

AND FOR YEARS AFTERWARDS...

ONE YEAR LATER...
A MUSICAL?
I THOUGHT YOU WERE THROUGH WITH PLAYS, ZORA.
THIS PRODUCTION WILL BE ALL MUSIC, GODMOTHER!

IT'S INSPIRED BY WHAT I SAW AND HEARD WHILE I WAS IN THE BAHAMAS...
THEIR CULTURE IS CLOSER TO ITS AFRICAN ROOTS THAN AMERICAN BLACK CULTURE IS.
THAT DOES SOUND INTRIGUING...
ONLY I DON'T RECALL GIVING YOU PERMISSION TO GO TO THE BAHAMAS...

VERY WELL. I'LL GIVE YOU SOME BACKING...
BUT YOU'LL HAVE TO COME UP WITH ADDITIONAL FUNDS ELSEWHERE.
YES, THAT'S WHY I'VE BEEN WRITING SKETCHES FOR ALL-NEGRO BROADWAY REVUES.

THAT'S A SELL OUT, ZORA...
I KNOW! BUT—
AND A DISTRACTION FROM YOUR REAL WORK.
I'M KNEE DEEP IN THIS SHOW ALREADY! I HAVE TO SEE IT THROUGH!
AND WE'VE YET TO GET PAID!

MARCH 29, 1932...
I'M SORRY YOUR SHOW WAS A FAILURE, ZORA...
"A FAILURE" ?!?
JUST LISTEN TO THAT APPLAUSE!
FROM SUN TO SUN
MUSIC FROM THE BAHAMAS

THE BOX OFFICE RECIEPTS TELL A DIFFERENT STORY.
AFTER ONLY ONE NIGHT?
WRITING IS YOUR TRUE CALLING, ZORA...
IT'S TIME YOU GOT BACK TO IT.
APPLAUSE
:SIGH: I CAN'T WIN!

SANFORD, FL, 1933...
LOOK AT ALL THESE **NOTES**!
I'VE COLLECTED MORE FOLKLORE THAN I KNOW WHAT TO **DO WITH**!
BOILING IT ALL DOWN TO ONE BOOK WILL BE **DAUNTING**!

BUT I'VE GOT TO GET IT DONE BEFORE **GOD-MOTHER** PASSES AWAY...
SHE'S IN **POOR HEALTH**, AND HURTING FINANCIALLY AS WELL...
I'LL NEVER SEE ANOTHER DIME FROM HER, BUT SHE'S GIVEN ME **PLENTY** THESE PAST SIX YEARS...

MY **OWN** HEALTH IS POOR, TOO...
MY BOWELS HAVE BEEN IN AN **UPROAR** EVER SINCE THAT TRIP TO THE BAHAMAS...
AND I CAN'T AFFORD THE **MEDICINE** FOR IT ANYMORE...

I CAN'T AFFORD **NEW SHOES**, EITHER... **OR** GROCERIES...
OR EVEN THE **RENT** ON THIS SHACK!
I NEED TO MAKE **MONEY**...
AS **ALWAYS**...

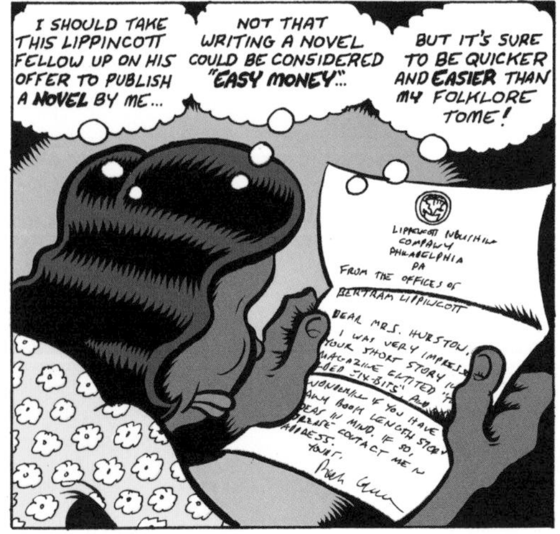
I SHOULD TAKE THIS LIPPINCOTT FELLOW UP ON HIS OFFER TO PUBLISH A **NOVEL** BY ME...
NOT THAT WRITING A NOVEL COULD BE CONSIDERED "**EASY MONEY**"...
BUT IT'S SURE TO BE QUICKER AND **EASIER** THAN MY FOLKLORE TOME!

I THINK I'LL WRITE A FICTIONALIZED ACCOUNT OF MY **PARENTS' LIVES**...
IT'LL BE IN KEEPING WITH MY NEW **LIFE MISSION**...
WHICH IS TO VALIDATE AND CELEBRATE MY **OWN PEOPLE**!

REACTIONS TO ZORA'S FIRST NOVEL, "JONAH'S GOURD VINE"...

THE HOME OF DANCER/ANTHROPOLOGIST KATHERINE DUNHAM, CHICAGO, 1935...

THANK YOU FOR HOSTING THIS PARTY FOR ME, KATHERINE!
IT'S MY PLEASURE, ZORA!
I'VE HEARD SO MUCH ABOUT YOU!
THOUGH YOU COULD HAVE AT LEAST SHOWN UP ON TIME!
ZORA!

I BELIEVE YOU KNOW PROFESSOR HERSKOVITS—
CONGRATULATIONS ON YOUR NEW FOLK-LORE COLLECTION, ZORA!
WHY, THANK YOU, PROFESSOR!

HMPF! ONE MINUTE THROUGH THE DOOR AND ALREADY SHE HAS THE ATTENTION OF ALL THE PROFESSORS I INVITED...
MY PROFESSORS!

HA HA HA!
OH, ZORA, YOU SLAY ME!
LOOK AT THEM! THEY'RE PUTTY IN HER HANDS!
THOUGH SHE IS PRETTIER THAN I THOUGHT SHE'D BE...
FOR AN OLD BROAD, THAT IS...

SOON...
I'M AFRAID I MUST RUN, KATHERINE...
BUT I WANTED TO ASK A FAVOR OF YOU...
OH?
A FAVOR? SOME NERVE!

I WAS HOPING I COULD USE YOUR PRACTICE SPACE FOR A SHOW OF MY OWN I'LL BE STAGING...
OH! BUT OF COURSE!

THANK YOU SO MUCH! I'LL BE IN TOUCH!
DON'T MENTION IT!
LAST TO ARRIVE, FIRST TO LEAVE...
AND NOW THIS!

:SIGH:
SHE'S MY HERO.

COLUMBIA UNIVERSITY, LATE 1935...

GOOD MORNING, MISS HURSTON!
?!?
DO I KNOW YOU?

I SANG IN ONE OF YOUR MUSICAL PRODUCTIONS YEARS AGO...
THE NAME'S PUNTER. PERCIVAL PUNTER.
PERCY! OF COURSE!
HOW COULD I FORGET A NAME LIKE THAT!
OR THAT PHYSIQUE! HUBBA HUBBA!
WHAT ARE YOU DOING HERE?

ATTENDING GRAD SCHOOL. HOW ABOUT YOU?
I'M SUPPOSED TO BE IN GRAD SCHOOL, BUT THEY JUST CUT MY SCHOLARSHIP IN HALF...
THEY SAID I HAVE TOO MUCH "PERSONALITY" TO BE A SERIOUS STUDENT...

...SO I'M GOING TO SKIP CLASS AND LIVE OFF OF MY HALF A GRANT WHILE I CONTINUE WRITING.
SO THEY'RE RIGHT—YOU AREN'T A SERIOUS STUDENT!
THOUGH I'VE ALWAYS ADMIRED THAT "BIG PERSONALITY" OF YOURS.

THREE MONTHS LATER...

AND SO...

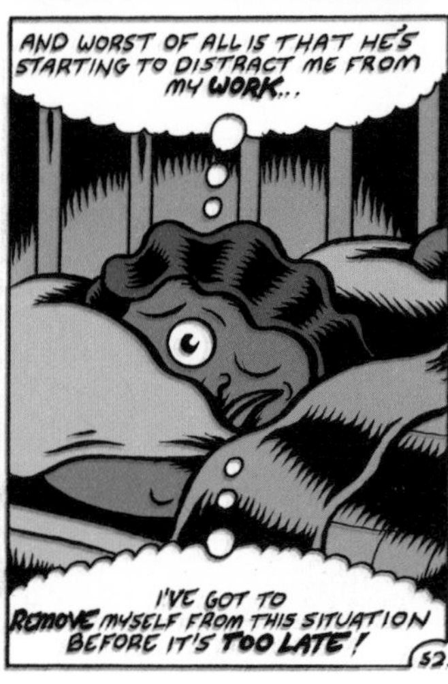

TOURING THE SOUTH AGAIN, THIS TIME WITH FELLOW FOLKLORIST ALAN LOMAX...

BAD NEWS, ZORA...
THE CHURCH WON'T LET US RECORD THEIR SERVICE AFTER ALL...
OH?
WE'LL SEE ABOUT THAT!

OH, BUT I DON'T WANT ANY TROUBLE. WE—
—YOU THERE! WAS I DREAMING, OR DID WE NOT COME TO AN UNDERSTANDIN' YESTERDAY?

WE DID NOT AGREE TO LET SOME CRACKER AND HIS CRAZY CONTRAPTION INTO OUR HOUSE OF WORSHIP!
WHERE IN THE SCRIPTURES IS THAT FOR-BIDDEN?
PLEASE SITE THE VERSE FOR ME!
ZORA, PLEASE! I—

YOU AND YO' YANKEE FRIEND CAN GO TO HELL!
I'M SURE YOU CAN SHOW US THE WAY!
AND HOW'D THE DEVIL BECOME GOD'S GATE-KEEPER?
WHOA! ZORA, DON'T—

JUST 'CUZ YOU'S SKIN-FOLK DON'T MAKE YOU KINFOLK!
AMEN TO THAT!
NOW MOVE, 'FORE I CUT ALL YO' HOLES INTO ONE BIG HOLE!
OH DEAR...
NOW SHE'S THREATENING TO USE VIOLENCE!

I'LL STOMP YO' GUTS OUT!
I'LL SHOOT YOU NICELY AND YOU'LL DIE POLITELY!
I'LL GUT YOU LIKE A PIG!
OH, THIS IS TERRIBLE!
MAYBE I SHOULD RUN AWAY...

—HEY, ALAN!
DRAG YO'SELF AND YO GIZMO IN HERE!
?
!

ZORA, YOU'RE AMAZING!
BUT, HOW?
I MEAN, YOU...

OH, I CAN OUT-NIGGER ANYBODY WHEN THE NEED ARISES.

LATER, BACK IN EATONVILLE...

JAMAICA, 1936: "I CONVINCED A GROUP OF MAROON TRIBESMEN TO TAKE ME ALONG ON A **WILD BOAR HUNT**...

"IT WAS ROUGH GOING, BUT I WAS DETERMINED TO SAMPLE THIS **ROASTED JERK PORK** I'D HEARD SO MUCH ABOUT!"

"THE MAROONS ARE FORMER SLAVES WHO ESCAPED TO THE ISLAND'S MOUNTAINOUS INTERIOR **CENTURIES** AGO...

"A UNIQUE CULTURE OF THEIR OWN EVOLVED — ALBEIT ONE THAT RETAINS MUCH OF THEIR **AFRICAN ROOTS**."

"THEY ALSO ALLOWED ME TO TAKE PART IN THEIR ELABORATE **MARITAL** AND **FUNERAL** RITUALS...

"AND I'D WITNESSED INEXPLICABLE **CONJURE DEMONSTRATIONS** BY A LOCAL WITCH DOCTOR."

I CAN'T HIDE MY CONTEMPT FOR **MAINSTREAM** JAMAICAN SOCIETY, HOWEVER...

"FOR EXAMPLE, THE RACISM THAT **LIGHT-SKINNED** NEGROES EXHIBIT TOWARD THEIR DARKER NEIGHBORS WOULD BE COMICAL IF IT WASN'T SO **PATHETIC**...

"WHILE THE DARKER-SKINNED WOMEN ARE TREATED AS LITTLE MORE THAN **PACK ANIMALS** DOWN HERE...

"IT MAKES ME GRATEFUL TO BE BORN AN **AMERICAN**!"

"MEANWHILE, I—

LATER, IN PORT-AU-PRINCE, HAITI...
"DEAR MR. LIPPINCOTT, I'M GLAD TO HEAR MY FOLKLORE COLLECTION IS SELLING WELL, AND HAS RECEIVED (MOSTLY) POSITIVE REVIEWS...
"THAT OUGHT TO BODE WELL FOR THE CARIBBEAN FOLK-LORE BOOK THAT I'M CURRENTLY WORKING ON..."

"AS WAS THE CASE IN JAMAICA, I'M COLLECTING MORE MATERIAL THAN I KNOW WHAT TO DO WITH...
"THE MORE I LEARN ABOUT VOODOO CULTURE, THE MORE I REALIZE I'M BARELY SCRATCHING THE SURFACE..."

"IT'S FAR MORE COMPLEX AND NUANCED THAN I COULD HAVE EVER POSSIBLY IMAGINED...
"AND THE VOLATILE POLITICAL SITUATION HERE MAKES RESEARCHING IT THAT MUCH MORE DIFFICULT..."

"IN THE MEANTIME, I'VE WRITTEN ANOTHER NOVEL, THE FIRST DRAFT OF WHICH I'M SENDING WITH THIS LETTER...
THEIR EYES WERE WATCHING GOD
By
Zora Neale Hurston
"I WROTE IT RATHER QUICKLY, IN AN ATTEMPT TO PROCESS MY FEELINGS OVER A RECENT BROKEN ROMANCE..."

"I'M SURE IT STILL NEEDS WORK, BUT I HOPE YOU'LL LIKE IT WELL ENOUGH TO CONSIDER PUBLISHING IT...
"IF SO, I COULD EASILY HAVE IT DONE BEFORE MY NEW FOLKLORE COLLECTION IS COMPLETED."

IF IT EVER IS COMPLETED, THAT IS...
I FEAR MY GASTRIC AILMENTS ARE SURE TO DO ME IN FIRST!

LATER, IN A HAITIAN HOSPITAL...
SO THIS WOMAN IS AN ACTUAL "ZOMBIE"?
WELL, SHE SHOWED UP RECENTLY AT THE FARM SHE GREW UP ON...

YET HER BROTHER SAID THEY HAD BURIED HER 30 YEARS AGO.
HOW IS THAT POSSIBLE?
IS IT POSSIBLE?

LEGEND HAS IT THE "BOCOR" GIVE THEIR VICTIMS A DRUG THAT CAUSES DEATH-LIKE SYMPTOMS.
LATER, THEY'LL REVIVE THE VICTIM, THOUGH SOME BRAIN DAMAGE USUALLY OCCURS IN THE INTERIM.

OFTEN RENDERING THEM SPEECHLESS, AND EASY TO MANIPULATE.
FASCINATING...

CAN I MEET A BOCOR?
AND PERHAPS APPRENTICE WITH ONE?
WHAT DRUG DO THEY USE—
WHOA!
TRUST ME, MISS HURSTON, THEY DO NOT TAKE KINDLY TO NOSY-BODIES.

BUT I'M WILLING TO UNDERGO THE INITIATION PROCESS...
ARE YOU WILLING TO KILL SOMEONE?
OR WATCH SOMEONE BE KILLED?
♪

IF YOU WERE WISE, YOU'D DROP THIS NOTION RIGHT NOW!
WELL, I'M STILL GOING TO MAKE INQUIRIES...
I'M TOO CURIOUS!

SOON AFTERWARD...
ARRGH! MY GUTS ARE ON FIRE!
LUCILLE! TAKE ME TO A TRAVEL AGENT IMMEDIATELY!
BUT YOUR VISA ISN'T UP UNTIL—

I DON'T CARE! SOMETHING TELLS ME I'VE ALREADY OVERSTAYED MY WELCOME!
♪

DINING OUT WITH HER PUBLISHERS, PHILADELPHIA, PA, 1938...

CROSS CITY, FL, 1939: MORE FOLKLORE HUNTING, THIS TIME FOR THE W.P.A., AND WITH WRITER STETSON KENNEDY...

HEY, ZORA!
GATHER ANYTHING INTERESTING HERE?
OH, YOU COULD SAY THAT...
AYCOCK + LINDSAY TURPENTINE CO

THOUGH IT'S HARDLY WHAT I WAS HOPING TO LEARN...
IN THAT THE EMPLOYEES AND THEIR FAMILIES ARE VIRTUAL SLAVES AT THIS CAMP.
SAY WHAT?
HOW SO?

THE MEN ARE ROUTINELY BEATEN OVER THE SLIGHTEST INFRACTIONS...
WHILE THE FOREMEN FORCE THEMSELVES ONTO THEIR WIVES...
GOOD GOD!

THOSE CAUGHT TRYING TO ESCAPE HAVE BEEN KILLED...
NOT THAT THERE'S ANYWHERE TO RUN TO IN THIS REMOTE LOCALE...
THEY'RE HOPING WE CAN GET THE WORD OUT.
DO THE COMPANY'S OWNERS KNOW OF THIS?

I INTEND TO WRITE TO THEM LATER...
THOUGH I DOUBT IT WILL BE NEWS TO THEM...
(PSST! AN ARMED FOREMAN IS COMING THIS WAY)...
(YOU'D BETTER HIGHTAIL IT WHILE I DISTRACT HIM.)

SAY, WHO WAS THAT COLORED GAL YOU WERE TALKING TO?
SHE SURE ASKS A LOT OF QUESTIONS.
SHE WORKS FOR ME...
WE'RE DOING RESEARCH FOR THE U.S. GOVERNMENT.

HUH. WELL, SHE DID SEEM PRETTY SMART...
I'D RECKON SHE'S ABOUT THREE-FIFTHS WHITE.
?!? "THREE-FIFTHS"?

THE NORTH CAROLINA COLLEGE FOR NEGROES, DURHAM, NC, 1940...
DIDN'T WE SEND PROFESSOR HURSTON A MEMO REMINDING HER OF OUR RULES REGARDING PROPER DRESS AND COMPORTMENT?
WE DID INDEED, SIR...
ONLY IT SEEMS SHE'S DISINCLINED TO READ MEMOS.
ADMINISTRATION BLDG.
SHE ALSO STILL REFUSES TO LIVE IN THE ON-CAMPUS HOUSING WE PROVIDE FOR OUR FEMALE EMPOYEES...
WHICH SHE REFERS TO AS A "PRISON".
OH, FOR GOODNESS' SAKE...
MEANWHILE, THERE'S ALSO BEEN RUMORS OF WILD GOINGS-ON AT THAT CABIN SHE'S RENTING...
OH? WELL, I HOPE THEY DON'T INVOLVE OTHER FACULTY MEMBERS...
FRATERNIZING WITH HER MALE COLLEAGUES WOULD BE IN VIOLATION OF HER CONTRACT.
I DON'T THINK SHE READS CONTRACTS EITHER, SIR...
BUT THAT'S NOT THE WORST OF IT...
SHE'S ALLEGEDLY HAVING AN AFFAIR WITH A MALE STUDENT AS WELL.
THAT DOES IT!
AS MUCH AS I LIKE HER PERSONALLY, I'M AFRAID I'M GOING TO HAVE TO—
J. E. SHEPARD
SIDENT
HAVE TO WHAT, SIR?
!!
MISS HURSTON, YOU'RE FIRED!
OH, I SEE...
I GUESS I WON'T HAVE TO BURDEN YOU WITH THIS LIST OF DEMANDS, THEN.

THE HOME OF ETHEL WATERS, HOLLYWOOD, CA, 1941...

PROMOTING HER NEW AUTOBIOGRAPHY, 1942 - '43...
YOUR NEW BOOK HAS LITTLE TO SAY ABOUT WORLD POLITICS...
OH, BUT ORIGINALLY IT HAD PLENTY TO SAY...
ABOUT THE EVILS OF COLONIALISM, AND THE FORCED IMPOSITION ON ANGLO CULTURE...
BUT NOW THAT WE'RE AT WAR MY PUBLISHER CUT IT ALL OUT...
"RALLY 'ROUND THE FLAG" AND ALL THAT...
DUST TRACKS ON A ROAD
YOU WERE QUOTED AS SAYING JIM CROW LAWS WORK?!
THEY "WORK" IN THAT A BLACK MAN KNOWS WHERE HE STANDS DOWN SOUTH...
WHILE RACISM IN THE NORTH IS UNPREDICTABLE AND ARBITRARY...
NEW YORK WORLD-TELEGRAM
BUT I DO NOT SUPPORT JIM CROW LAWS!
THEY'RE CRUEL AND UNJUST!
AND IF WHITES REALLY ARE THE "SUPERIOR" RACE THEN WHY THE NEED TO STACK THE DECK IN THEIR FAVOR?
SO YOU DO OPPOSE SEGREGATION.
I OPPOSE FORCED SEGREGATION...
PEOPLE SHOULD BE FREE TO CHOSE WHERE THEY LIVE AND WORK...
WNBC
BUT THIS INCLUDES THE FREEDOM TO LIVE WITH YOUR OWN KIND...
BLACK AMERICANS HAVE A DISTINCT CULTURE THAT I FEAR INTEGRATION WOULD DILUTE—OR EVEN OBLITERATE...
AND IT'S SOMETHING I FEEL IS WORTH PRESERVING.
BUT MANY WHITE LIBERALS FEEL THAT—
WHITE LIBERALISM IS ANOTHER FORM OF RACISM...
THEY PRESUME I NEED THEIR HELP TO GET AHEAD...
AND THAT I "OWE" THEM IN RETURN!
WE CAN "UPLIFT" OURSELVES BY OURSELVES...
LIKE I'VE BEEN DOING SINCE I WAS THIRTEEN...
ALL I ASK OF WHITES IS TO GET OUT OF MY WAY!

HARLEM, NY, 1946...
BY WORKING IN SHIFTS, YOU'LL ALL HAVE FREE DAY CARE SEVEN DAYS A WEEK!
BUT CONGRESSMAN POWELL SAYS THAT GOVERNMENT SHOULD PROVIDE US WITH FREE DAY CARE.
THE HARLEM BLOCK MOTHERS' COMMITTEE
HOW GENEROUS OF HIM!
AND WHAT ARE Y'ALL GONNA DO IN THE MEANTIME?
AT LEAST WE WON'T BE DOING THE BABYSITTING OURSELVES.
YOU'D RATHER HAVE STRANGERS RAISE YOUR KIDS?
AND WHO ARE SURE TO CRITICIZE YOUR OWN PARENTING SKILLS?
HMPF.
HMMM...
BESIDES, THIS WILL GIVE YOU A CHANCE TO SOCIALIZE MORE!
WELL, I FOR ONE HAVE FAITH IN ADAM CLAYTON POWELL, JR.!
AND I ATTEND HIS CHURCH REGULAR!
THAT'S HIS FATHER'S CHURCH!
POWELL SENIOR IS A GOOD MAN...
JUNIOR, ON THE OTHER HAND, IS JUST A SELF-SERVING PLAYBOY!
ALL THE MORE REASON TO VOTE FOR HIS OPPONENT, GRANT REYNOLDS, THIS NOVEMBER...
HE'S A GOOD MAN TOO!
?!? HE'S A REPUBLICAN!
VOTE FOR GRANT REYNOLDS FOR U.S. CONGRESS
MY HUSBAND SAYS TO ONLY VOTE FOR DEMOCRATS FROM NOW ON...
REALLY? WITH ALL THEIR EMPTY PROMISES?
IT'S BETTER THAN WHAT THE G.O.P. IS PROMISING—WHICH IS NOTHING!

PUERTO CORTÉS, HONDURAS, 1947...
I DON'T THINK MY GUGGENHEIM GRANT IS GOING TO LAST VERY LONG IN THIS COUNTRY...
THE INFLATION DOWN HERE IS BRUTALIZING MY WALLET!

HOPEFULLY MY NEW PUBLISHER WILL GIVE ME A SECOND ADVANCE ONCE THEY'VE SEEN THE FIRST DRAFT OF MY NEW NOVEL...
OTHERWISE I'LL NEVER BE ABLE TO VISIT THE INTERIOR OF THIS COUNTRY LIKE I HAD PLANNED TO...

IT PAINS ME TO NOT BE WORKING WITH LIPPINCOTT ANY-MORE, BUT I COULDN'T TURN DOWN THE CHANCE TO WORK WITH SCRIBNER'S...
AND ESPECIALLY WITH THE LEGENDARY MAXWELL PERKINS —THE GREATEST LITERARY EDITORY IN THE WORLD!

HE'S EVEN AGREED TO LET ME WRITE A BOOK ABOUT WHITE PROTAGONISTS— A HUGE RISK FOR BOTH OF US!
KNOCK
KNOCK
MAIL FOR YOU, SEÑORA!

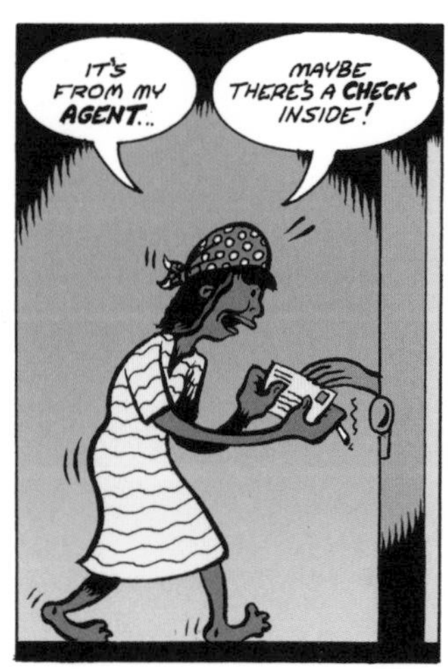
IT'S FROM MY AGENT...
MAYBE THERE'S A CHECK INSIDE!

OH NO...
MAX PERKINS IS DEAD...

WHY DO I SUDDENLY FEEL LIKE MY LIFE IS ABOUT TO UNRAVEL?

NEW YORK CITY, NY, SEPT., 1948...
MISS ZORA NEALE HURSTON?
WE HAVE A WARRANT FOR YOUR ARREST...
ARREST?! WHAT'S THE CHARGE?

CHILD MOLESTATION.
WHAT?!
YOU CAN'T BE SERIOUS!

LATER, AT THE LOCAL PRECINCT...
YOUR FORMER LANDLORD CLAIMS YOU'VE BEEN MOLESTING HER TEN-YEAR-OLD SON AND HIS FRIENDS FOR THE PAST YEAR...
THAT'S IMPOSSIBLE!

I WAS IN HONDURAS ALL YEAR!

LOOK! HERE'S MY PASSPORT!
HMMM...
IT SAYS YOU WERE BACK IN NEW YORK ON AUGUST 15...

YES! FOR ONE DAY!
EN ROUTE TO UPSTATE TO VISIT FRIENDS!
MAY I GO NOW?!
I'M AFRAID NOT...
YOU STILL HAVE TO APPEAR BEFORE A JUDGE TOMORROW.

THE NEXT DAY...
THE DEFENDANT ABUSED MY SON ON... UH, AUGUST 15...
OBJECTION, YOUR HONOR!
THIS WITNESS JUST COMPLETELY ALTERED HER TESTIMONY!

SHE NOW IS RELYING SOLELY ON THE INFORMATION MY CLIENT JUST GAVE THE POLICE YESTERDAY...
SHE'S EVEN READING FROM A SCRIPT!
THIS IS CLEARLY A SET UP!
DULY NOTED...
NEXT WITNESS...
BUT YOUR HONOR-
NEXT WITNESS!
THIS CAN'T BE HAPPENING!

MONTHS LATER, WITH CARLO AND FANNIE HURST...
...THE BOY CLAIMED THAT I— AND TWO OTHER ADULTS I DON'T EVEN KNOW— ROUTINELY LED HIM AND HIS FRIENDS INTO A BASEMENT AND PERFORMED ORAL SEX ON THEM...
WHY, THAT'S INSANE!
IT TURNS OUT HE AND HIS FRIENDS WERE "EXPERIMENTING" WITH EACH OTHER...
FEARFUL OF GETTING CAUGHT, THEY BEGAN TO POINT FINGERS.
BUT WHY WOULD HE ACCUSE YOU?
THE BOY WAS ALWAYS TROUBLED, AND I ADVISED HIS MOTHER TO GET HIM HELP...
SHE RESENTED ME FOR THAT, AND THE BOY KNEW IT, SO I WAS AN EASY TARGET.
WELL, AT LEAST IT'S ALL OVER NOW...
OH, I DOUBT I'LL EVER GET OVER THIS...
I FEEL SO... ABANDONED.
NONSENSE, ZORA!
WE DIDN'T DOUBT YOUR INNOCENCE FOR A SINGLE SECOND!
I KNOW, I KNOW...
BUT WHAT ABOUT MY BLACK FRIENDS!
WHERE ARE MY OWN PEOPLE?
WELL, THAT HARLEM MOTHERS COMMITTEE YOU HELPED ORGANIZE SPOKE OUT ON YOUR BEHALF...
I MEAN MY PEERS! LANGSTON AND THE REST!
THEIR SILENCE IS DEAF-ENING!
IS IT BECAUSE I'M NOT A COMMUNIST LIKE THEY ARE?
OH, NOW, ZORA...
AND THE BLACK PRESS ASSUMED I WAS GUILTY EVEN AFTER I'D BEEN CLEARED...
HOW AM I SUPPOSED TO PROMOTE MY NEW BOOK NOW?
I'M AFRAID TO SHOW MY FACE!
:SIGH.:
BOTH MY COUNTRY AND MY RACE HAVE FAILED ME...
I JUST WANT TO CRAWL INTO A HOLE AND DIE.

ABOARD A FRIEND'S CARGO SHIP, MIAMI, FL, 1950...
GOD NEVER FAILS TO PAINT A MASTERPIECE IN THE FLORIDA SKIES AT NIGHT...
BEING BACK HERE MAKES ME FEEL LIKE MYSELF AGAIN.

BUT I'M ALSO BACK TO MY USUAL PROBLEM: BEING BROKE...
MY ROYALTIES ARE BEING GOBBLED UP BY MY LEGAL BILLS...
I'M GONNA HAVE TO FIND A JOB... ANY JOB...

AND SOON!

AND SO...
THE JOB PAYS $30 A WEEK, PLUS ROOM AND BOARD...
CAN YOU COOK?
I'M AN EXCELLENT COOK.
GOOD. YOU'RE HIRED!

SHORTLY...
?!?
ZORA, ARE YOU BY ANY CHANCE THE SAME WOMAN WHO WROTE THIS ARTICLE I'M READING?
INDEED I AM, MA'AM.
SATURDAY EVENING POST

SOON...
MY MAID IS SIMPLY ONE OF THE MOST INTERESTING PEOPLE I'VE EVER MET...
YOU REALLY SHOULD INTERVIEW HER FOR YOUR NEWSPAPER!
UH OH.

INEVITABLY...
I'M DOING RESEARCH FOR A PIECE ON THE LIVES OF DOMESTIC WORKERS...
PLUS I COULD USE THE EXERCISE, HA HA!
HA HA!
GOOD! HE BOUGHT IT!

THE RUBY McCOLLUM MURDER TRIAL, LIVE OAK, FL, 1952...

SO YOU ADMIT TO SHOOTING DR. ADAMS...
YES, BUT I—
THAT IS ALL, YOUR HONOR.

YOUR HONOR, THE DEFENSE WOULD LIKE TO ENTER NEW EVIDENCE—
YOU MAY NOT.
BUT YOUR HONOR, THERE ARE MITIGATING CIRCUMSTANCES THAT—
MOTION DENIED!
(WHITE VICTIM, BLACK SUSPECT)...
(SHE DOESN'T STAND A CHANCE.)

(STILL, SERVES HER RIGHT, GETTIN' MIXED UP WIT' A WHITE MAN 'N' ALL...)
(WHAT DE HELL WAS SHE THINKING?)
(AMEN TO THAT.)
LISTEN TO THESE TWO HENS...

DO THEY REALLY BELIEVE WHAT THEY'RE SAYING?
OR IS IT JUST TO APPEASE ANY WHITE PERSON WITHIN EARSHOT?
(I THOUGHT YO' HUSBAND WAS COMIN' TODAY...)
(HE WAS, TILL HE SAW ALL THEM KLANSMEN OUTSIDE)...
(SO HE WENT FISHIN' INSTEAD, HAW HAW!)

BESIDES, EVERYONE KNEW THE VICTIM WAS HARDLY A SAINT...
THOUGH NO ONE DARES TO GO ON RECORD SAYING AS MUCH...
(HEY! WHATCHOO WRITIN'?)
(YOU A REPORTER?)

(YES, I'M COVERING THE TRIAL FOR THE PITTSBURGH COURIER.)
('ZAT SO? I HOPE YOU WON'T BE TOO KIND TO THE DEFENDANT)...
...(SINCE SHE DON'T DESERVE IT!)

(PERHAPS NOT, BUT SHE AT LEAST PUTS MY OWN PROBLEMS IN PERSPECTIVE.)
(HMMM... GOOD POINT.)

NEAR EAU GALLIE, FL, 1955...

SO, ZORA, I READ YOUR LETTER TO THE EDITOR CRITICIZING THE **BROWN V. BOARD OF EDUCATION** DECISION...

UH **HUH**...

SEEMS LIKE THE **WHOLE WORLD'S** READ IT BY NOW...

IT'S CAUSED QUITE A **STIR**.

BUT HOW COULD YOU OPPOSE **INTEGRATION**?

I **DON'T**...

I OPPOSE **FORCED** INTEGRATION...

AS WELL AS **GOVERNMENT-IMPOSED** SEGREGATION!

BUT THE NEGRO SCHOOLS ARE SO **UNDER-FUNDED**...

THEN **FULLY FUND** THEM! PROBLEM **SOLVED**!

"**SPEND**, DON'T **BLEND**": THAT'S WHAT MOST BLACK EDUCATORS **REALLY** WANT.

STILL, THE NEGRO STUDENTS WOULD SURELY **BENEFIT**—

**HOW?** SIMPLY BY BEING IN THE PRESENCE OF **WHITE** STUDENTS?

AND THE POORER BLACK KIDS WILL BE TREATED LIKE **DIRT**, WHAT WITH THEIR **SHABBY CLOTHES** AND **BAD HYGIENE** AND ALL.

IN BLACK SCHOOLS, THE BEST AND BRIGHTEST ARE GROOMED FOR **GREATNESS**...

WHILE AT A WHITE SCHOOL THEY'LL **ALL** BE GROOMED TO BE **JANITORS**.

I SEE YOUR POINT, BUT **STILL**...

AT THE HOME OF ARTIST "BEANIE" BACKUS, FORT PIERCE, FL, 1958...
YEAH! PLAY IT, BOYS!
EXCUSE ME, BUT ARE YOU ZORA NEALE HURSTON?
THEE ZORA HURSTON?
WHO WANTS TO KNOW?
I'M MARJORIE SILVER, A LOCAL RADIO BROAD-CASTER...
I USED TO READ YOUR WORK BACK IN MY NEW YORK DAYS!

YOU'RE ALLOWED TO READ IT DOWN HERE TOO, YOU KNOW.
HA HA! TRUE, ONLY YOU HAVEN'T WRITTEN A BOOK IN A WHILE, IT SEEMS.
I'VE BEEN WORKING ON A NEW ONE FOR YEARS, ABOUT KING HEROD.
?!? THE BIBLICAL BABY KILLER?
HE WAS A GREAT MAN! AND UNFAIRLY MALIGNED!
BUT I FEAR I'VE BEEN WASTING MY TIME, SINCE I CAN'T FIND A PUBLISHER.
LISTEN, I HAVE A LOT OF CONTACTS IN PUBLISHING...
AND I'M HEADING BACK UP NORTH THIS WEEK...

IF YOU'D LIKE, I COULD TAKE THE MANUSCRIPT WITH ME AND SHOW IT AROUND...
WOULD YOU? I'D SO APPRECIATE IT!
SOON...
THIS LONG TRAIN RIDE WILL GIVE ME PLENTY OF TIME TO READ ZORA'S MANUSCRIPT...
FORT PIERCE

HOURS LATER...
OH DEAR...
THIS BOOK IS A MESS!
SHE'S LOST IT!

THE HOME OF ZORA'S LANDLORD, DR. C.C. BENTON, FORT PIERCE, FL, 1959...

FORT PIERCE, FL, 1973...
ARE YOU SURE THIS IS THE RIGHT PLACE, ALICE?
IT LOOKS ABANDONED.
THIS IS WHERE THE FOLKS AT THE MORTUARY SAID IT WAS...
THOUGH HOW WE'LL FIND THE GRAVE IS BEYOND ME.
HOW YOU'LL FIND IT, YOU MEAN...
I'M NOT GOING IN THERE...
THERE'S SURE TO BE SNAKES IN THERE!
SNAKES?!
THANKS FOR NOTHING, CHARLOTTE!

WELL, I'VE COME THIS FAR...
NO TURNING BACK NOW...
THOUGH HOW AM I SUPPOSED TO FIND AN UNMARKED GRAVE?

THIS SUNKEN RECTANGLE HAS NO MARKINGS...
IT MIGHT BE THE ONE...
AND AT THIS POINT, WHAT DIFFERENCE DOES IT MAKE?

HOW DID IT COME TO THIS?
A LITERARY GENIUS, ALL BUT FORGOTTEN...
WITH A GRAVE LEFT UNATTENDED FOR 13 YEARS...

AND SO...
WELL? WHAT NOW?
WE'RE GOING TO BUY A TOMBSTONE!
END!

# WHO, WHAT, WHERE, WHEN AND WHY

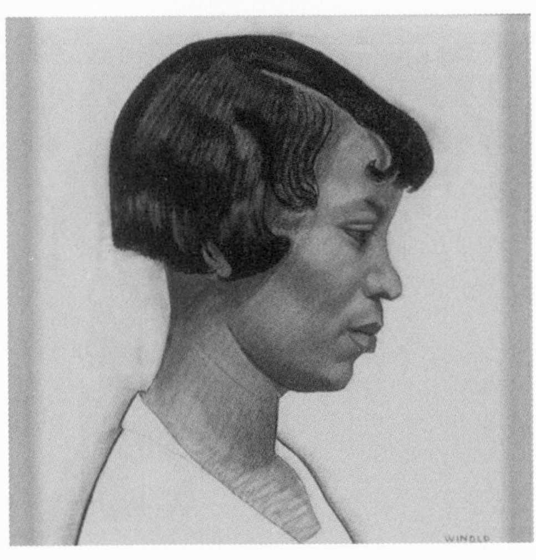

ABOVE
*Hurston, as portrayed by the German-born artist (and Harlem habitué) Winold Reiss, circa 1925. Reiss may have taken liberties with Hurston's hairdo here, since she's never been photographed wearing her hair this short.*

PAGES 1 AND 2
Zora Neale Hurston was born in Notasulga, Alabama, on January 7, 1891. It is unknown where her parents got the name "Zora" from (or her middle name, which originally was spelled "Neal" until she later feminized it by adding the extra e). Her parents, John and Lucy Hurston, were both Notasulga natives, and her grandparents were all born into slavery.

Her father's family were poor sharecroppers, and John Hurston himself was rumored to be the illegitimate son of the local plantation owner, which would explain his green eyes and very light skin (in *Jonah's Gourd Vine*, Hurston's barely fictionalized retelling of her parents' story, John's white biological father showed him favor by giving him clothes, preferred jobs on his farm, etc.). John Hurston was also extremely ambitious and resourceful, which he had to be in order to win the hand of Lucy Potts, daughter of a prosperous farmer, and a member of the town's leading Black family.

Gainfully employed as a highly skilled carpenter, John Hurston moved his young family to the small, all-Black town of Eatonville, located just north of Orlando, in 1893 (though not too common, there were quite a few all-Black towns in the South by this time, particularly in Florida). John quickly became one of the town's leaders, and frequently served as the town's mayor. Possessing impressive oratory skills, John also became a popular preacher, and greatly added to his income by serving as a guest preacher to Baptist congregations throughout central Florida.

Hurston grew up in a well-maintained eight-bedroom home on a seven-acre lot that produced more food than her large family could eat (she and her siblings used to indulge in egg fights when they were little). Being a monoracial town also meant Hurston was exposed to very little racial strife while growing up—the only societal conflicts centered around whether you were a Baptist or a Methodist—though she certainly grew to be aware of the town's precarious existence (in fact, another all-Black town, Rosewood, FL, was completely destroyed by neighboring whites in 1923, in response to a false rape allegation). Still, Eatonville was so peaceful that it had no police department, or even a jail. Troublemakers were simply encouraged to leave town!

John and Lucy Hurston had nine children, eight of whom survived to adulthood. In age order (with estimated birth years), they were:

1882: Hezekiah Robert (Bob)
1883: Isaac (died in childhood)
1885: John Cornelius
1887: Richard William (Dick)
1889: Sarah Emmeline
1891: Zora Neale
1893: Clifford Joel
1895: Benjamin Franklin
1898: Everett Edward

All of the surviving boys did quite well for themselves as adults, pursuing solid, recession-proof careers (doctor, grocer, chef, high school principal, pharmacist, and postman, respectively). Hurston's lone sister, Sarah, married a preacher at a young age but often had to take in lodgers or sell meals from her own kitchen to make ends meet. Sarah's lack of autonomy (as well as her mother's) had a huge impact on her younger sister, and fueled Hurston's determination to remain economically independent.

ABOVE
*Eatonville, FL, councilmen, 1907. None of the men pictured are identified.*

PAGE 3
Along with her own father, Joe Clarke was Eatonville's other leading figure during Hurston's childhood, and his general store doubled as the town's social center. Both Clarke and his store remained a fixture in many of Hurston's future writings. The story being told here might have been too ribald to be shared in a child's presence, but the young Hurston was too curious not to listen in on *everything* being said on that store's porch.

PAGES 4 AND 5
Fictionalized versions of Hurston's maternal grandmother were also a fixture in many of her stories, in which she plays the role of the heavy-handed, judgmental disciplinarian. It's ironic that Grandma Potts never got over her loathing for her son-in-law, since both of them wanted to take a switch to Zora for her fanciful ways.

Even more ironic (not to mention tragic) is the way her father favored her older sister, since Hurston resembled her father in almost every way: the broad facial features, the solid frame, the bold, ambitious personality. This left a permanent scar on Hurston's psyche, since even though she "knew" she was beautiful (and was told as much often enough), she still would often think of herself as "ugly" well into late middle age.

Popular itinerant preachers were the equivalent of rock stars at such a place and time, so it'd come as no surprise that Hurston's father had many "groupies" along his circuit.

HIGH YELLOW (OR 'YALLER'): A light-skinned Negro. Possessing lighter skin would soon become much desired (and highly politicized) among African-Americans in the early twentieth century, but to a former slave like Granny Potts, it was also almost certain proof that you were sired by a white man, and thus born out of wedlock. Thus, the terms "high yellow" and "bastard" were practically synonymous.

FROM OVER THE CREEK: A phrase that meant the same thing as "from the wrong side of the tracks," and that (obviously) predates the arrival of the locomotive.

PAGES 6 AND 7
Hurston's mother died when she was thirteen. This event thoroughly traumatized Hurston, so much so that one has to question the accuracy of how she described these and later events. While it's safe to assume that Lucy Hurston was a wonderful woman, her daughter describes her as nothing less than a saint, while other players come off as pure evil in comparison. Alas, there are no other sources available to tell us if the situation really was that black and white, though those that did know her mother found it hard to believe that she'd reject her own deeply held Baptist beliefs on her deathbed.

Being a self-described tomboy, the young Hurston disliked store-bought dolls—she used to hurl them off of rooftops, or "drown" them until they confessed to where the gold was buried, all while her sister would be serving her doll tea—and instead preferred acting out involved dramas with her own play figures made out of found objects like corn pones or bars of soap.

LEFT
*John Hurston, circa late 1900s. Hurston's father had relocated with his new wife to nearby Sanford, FL, by then. No pictures exist of Hurston's mother, Lucy.*

PAGE 8
The rapidity with which Hurston's family disintegrated in the wake of her mother's death was mind-boggling, yet predictable in retrospect. In the years leading up to Hurston's mother's death, the Hurstons were widely regarded as

Eatonville's leading "power couple," with Lucy being as much loved and respected—indeed, even more so—as her husband. She taught Sunday school, gave music lessons, nursed the sick, fed the poor—heck, maybe she *was* a saint! Sadly, the only person who failed to appreciate his wife's virtues by this time was John Hurston himself, who had become so full of himself that he no longer recognized the role his wife played in his success (Hurston often compared her father's rise and fall to that of the mythological Icarus). The oldest sons were already attending school elsewhere, and the exit soon became a stampede when their father married one of his former groupies: the much despised Mattie Moge. This also led to a stampede from John's own pews, since no one wanted to be preached to by someone who was quickly becoming a laughing stock. Indeed, John Jr. came very close to assaulting his father as he walked out the door for the last time.

Meanwhile, Sarah Hurston's favored daughter status suddenly turned into a booby prize, since her new (and barely five years older) stepmother regarded her as a rival for her father's affections. Too accustomed to being a daddy's girl, Sarah immediately married an obvious stand-in: a much older man who also happened to be a preacher. Unfortunately, Sarah's new husband lacked her father's oratory (and money-making) skills.

PAGE 9

Hurston was actually a bit vague about whether she acquiesced to this (or any other) employer's sexual demands. This one character must have stuck out in her memory simply for the scattershot romantic desperation he exhibited. Sadly, enduring and/or giving in to the "master's" come-ons was an occupational hazard for domestic help in those bad old days, and it was surely the main reason she wound up avoiding that line of work.

PAGE 10 AND 11

Hurston almost certainly elaborated on this story somewhat—what with those *expertly thrown kitchen knives* and all—though it certainly illustrates what a low point her life had reached. While she had no idea what to do with herself by that point, she certainly knew that she didn't want to remain some brawlin' backwoods betty for the rest of her life, and the way she gave into her basest animal instincts at this moment thoroughly mortified her (though Hurston also could barely hide at least some glee while recalling turning her hated stepmother's face into hamburger meat, even thirty years after the fact).

This story also illustrates Hurston's visceral "fight or flight" instinct, and her lifelong, not always successful determination to overcome it. It also shows what, among other things, she hoped to obtain from a higher education: the mind-over-matter discipline to view situations objectively, rather than to respond to them with pure emotion. Hurston was a hypersensitive woman who possessed a tremendous capacity for love as well as hate, but she needed to find a way to channel those feelings in a way that wouldn't lead to disaster. So it's no surprise that she became an artist, and a powerful one at that.

In defense of the much maligned Mattie Moge: I'd say her biggest flaw was her naïveté: the way she assumed she could step into Lucy Hurston's shoes (and her *bed*—how symbolic was *that?*) without any blowback. But she was young, and her husband certainly should have foreseen all this. In fact, John Hurston obviously misled her as to what to expect when he brought her home. So much—if not all—of the rage Zora exhibited here should have been directed at her father instead.

LEFT
*Hurston (L) with her brother Bob and his family, Memphis, TN, 1912–13. This, as far as I know, is the only existing photo taken of Hurston during the first twenty-five years of her life.*

PAGES 12 AND 13

At the risk of belaboring the obvious: the conventional wisdom of the day was that pursuing a higher education (or even a high school diploma) was little more than a luxury for women, particularly to Hurston's pragmatic-minded brothers (who were clearly *raised* to be pragmatic, and who also felt it was their duty to keep their sister chaste until she *was* married. Even if she were to get a job as a teacher or a nurse, chances were more than likely that she'd get married and have children eventually anyway, so why invest the time and money?

Twenty years after this scene took place, Bob Hurston apologized to his sister (by then a college graduate and professional writer) for underestimating her desire to resume and complete her education. Of course, by then it was obvious that she had no intention of living a conventional life, either!

The only record of Hurston's existence over the ten-year period starting from when she left her father's home for good (euphemistically referred to as her "lost years") was when she signed her name into the registry of the Bethel Baptist Church in Jacksonville. Biographer Valerie Boyd points out that it was relatively easy for anyone—and particularly a Black woman—to "disappear" from any and all public records back then, but during the next two years, she disappeared not only from her own family's sight, but even from her own official memory.

PAGE 14
The text on this page was all taken (and shamelessly edited down by yours truly) from a passage from Hurston's autobiography, *Dust Tracks on a Road*. The two middle panels cover literally all that she's ever shared regarding a roughly two-year period, from late 1914 to early 1916—the *truly* lost years of her "lost years" period. What's clearly implied is that she lived with a man (there's no record of a marriage, so it must have been a common-law arrangement) during this time, and that it wasn't a pleasant experience. In fact, her use of the word "torture" makes it difficult not to assume the worst: that she experienced physical and/or verbal abuse from this man, who also may well have been the role model for the various domestic tyrants that populate some of her fiction. She also specifically mentions betrayal, but then it didn't take much for Hurston to feel betrayed (as will be covered later). Then again, her sense of shame and recalcitrance in discussing this episode could also partially (solely?) be due to her temporarily abandoning the pursuit of her much cherished and hard-won autonomy, and that her use of the word "torture" was, at least to some degree, hyperbole (something that Hurston was no stranger to). Alas, we'll never know for sure.

At this point I must mention that the similarities between Hurston and the subject of my last biography, Margaret Sanger, are uncanny, and not only because their lives paralleled each other: both came from large, productive families; both led multifaceted, ever-evolving lives; both had an inner drive that others found both inspiring and frightening; both were sexually liberated, and had ambivalent feelings at best toward marriage; both wrote prolifically on countless topics; both successfully lied to the world about their ages; both followed no religion but possessed a profound sense of spirituality; and weirdest of all, both women put tremendous stock in their own dreams and visions, to the point of turning to them for guidance!

One thing these two women *do not* have in common, however, is that Hurston never once discussed what was Sanger's forte: birth control. Hurston had no children, and she never mentioned, either publicly or privately, being pregnant. Did she use *some* form of birth control? Or was she simply unable to conceive? Her other biographers never even broach this topic, but it's hard not to contemplate what a potentially huge turn her life might have taken if she had had children.

ABOVE
*A 1908 production of H.M.S. Pinafore.*

PAGES 15 AND 16
Besides being Hurston's first step out of the hole she'd long been in, her joining this theater company was her first full introduction into the multifaceted world of *white people*, and the many sub-categories therein: Irish, Jews, Italians, etc., along with the many stereotypes ascribed to each. Fortunately for her, theater folks are and were far more open-minded than the regular population, so all their ethnic ribbing was largely good-natured (not to mention their general acceptance of non-conventional forms of sexuality, which must have been an eye-opener for her). Hurston's new colleagues also couldn't get enough of her southern-fried stories and dialect, and would fight to sit next to her during their long train rides. That also must have been an eye-opener—that there was a potential *audience* for her Eatonville yarns!

Hurston never got over her "theater bug," and spent the rest of her life struggling to remain involved with the stage. The "sass" that Hurston is shown dishing out on panel six of page 15 is a mere sampling of a long paragraph's worth of insults she used to illustrate the way Eatonville-ites would "play the dozens."

Hurston never identified her employer, the young ingénue "Miss M"—which is curious, since she only had positive things to say about her.

Not only did Hurston get away with shaving ten years off of her age in order to enroll in high school, but she got away with that deceit for the rest of her life and beyond. (Even her first biographer, Robert Hemenway, assumed she was born in 1901, since there was no known evidence at the time to prove otherwise.) In fact, she would later sometimes shave fifteen or even twenty years off of her age—depending, presumably, on the age of the man she was trying to woo at the time.

PAGE 17 AND 18
As shown here, the motivated Hurston excelled academically. The only thing that slowed her down throughout her academic career was the annoying need to make a living, which often *did* affect her grades once she entered Howard. The end result was that she wound up on the "ten year plan," since it wasn't until 1928 that she finally earned her college diploma. Curiously, the one subject she routinely failed at Howard was physical education (which was required at the time). Hurston was by all accounts quite athletic, yet she simply didn't show up for class. But then, who *doesn't* hate gym? Howard also modeled its curriculum on Harvard's, where Latin was still a required course, along with the dreaded Classical Greek.

Hurston occasionally made half-baked attempts at starting her own business—even at the height of her career she seriously considered starting a fried chicken catering service, since she felt New York City was in dire need of some decent Southern food—only to be reminded that she wasn't cut out for the financial and accounting end of being an entrepreneur.

Hurston's father eventually split with his second wife Mattie, and—by then a very broken man—lived with various sons, eventually staying with Bob in Memphis, which is where he died. There's no record of Hurston considering his death a possible suicide, though the thought of a fifty-seven-year-old teetotaler playing chicken with a freight train in the middle of the night sure sounds...odd.

Hurston did not attend her father's funeral.

LEFT
*Hurston's yearbook photo, date unknown.*

DR. ALAIN LOCKE (1885–1954) was the first African-American Rhodes scholar, and graduated from Harvard with a PhD in philosophy. He's widely regarded as the "dean" of the Harlem Renaissance movement, and devoted much of his life to promoting young Black artists and authors. Locke was also unambiguously gay, as well as a notorious misogynist, which his female students naturally assumed were intrinsically linked. While he did exhibit ridiculously unfair favoritism to his male students, he also made a notable exception with Hurston, and served as a mentor of sorts for her off and on for the next fifteen years. Their relationship often proved to be a testy one, however—and it reached its nadir when a condescending review Locke wrote of *Their Eyes Were Watching God* threw Hurston into such a rage that she claimed to have seriously considered murdering him!

PAGE 19
Illinois native HERBERT ARNOLD SHEEN (1897–?) entered Harvard after serving in the army during WWI. He and Hurston's relationship, though sexual, was mostly friendly and casual, with the subject of marriage popping up only intermittently. Sheen's sister (whom Hurston knew) was murdered by her husband while they were still at Howard, and Hurston did much to help him and his family cope through that horrific ordeal. This, according to Sheen, created a permanent, deep bond between the two of them, so while the nature of their relationship went through changes, they remained very close to the end of her days.

LEFT TO RIGHT
*"Race leaders" Alain Locke, Charles S. Johnson, and W. E. B. Du Bois, all photos circa the 1920s.*

PAGE 20
*Opportunity* magazine was associated with the National Urban League, and published that organization's sociological studies regarding Black American life, along with art, fiction, poetry, and essays by Black writers. Its editor, CHARLES S. JOHNSON (1893–1956), adhered to the Booker T. Washington lift-yourself-up-by-your-own-bootstraps school of Negro Advancement, and this conservative approach (especially in contrast to W. E. B. Du Bois's far more militant *The Crisis* magazine), along with its multiracial board of directors, made it an increasing target of left-wing criticism as time went on. Still, Johnson was fondly remembered by all for the way he and his wife routinely opened their Harlem home to newcomers, and for then helping them find permanent lodgings.

PAGE 21
The *Opportunity*-sponsored event portrayed here has often been described as the Harlem Renaissance's "coming out party," in that it suddenly made everyone aware that Harlem's unique, burgeoning arts culture was, indeed, a "thing." The attendees pictured in the first panel, from left to right, are:

GWENDOLYN BENNETT (1902–1981): Artist, poet, and (at the time) *Opportunity*'s art director.

H.L. MENCKEN (1880–1956): Journalist, critic, and coeditor of the new *The American Mercury*, seen talking to…

JEAN TOOMER (1894–1967): Poet and novelist.

Behind CHARLES S. JOHNSON (in glasses, speaking to ALAIN LOCKE) is…

CASPER HOLSTEIN (1876–1944): Harlem based mobster and "numbers king." He financially supported many Harlem artists, and helped to bankroll this very shindig.

EUGENE O'NEILL (1888–1953): Playwright.

PAUL ROBESON (1898–1976): Singer, actor, and political activist, along with his wife…

ESLANDA ROBESON (1895–1965): Her husband's manager, and (later) anthropologist.

W. E. B. DU BOIS (1868–1963): Sociologist, activist, author, editor, cofounder of the NAACP.

CARL VAN VECHTEN (1880–1964): (Then) Critic and novelist, talking to his wife…

FANIA MARINOFF (1890–1971): Dancer, actress, and model. Behind her is…

JESSIE FAUSET (1882–1961): Writer, teacher, and then-literary editor of *The Crisis*. Behind her is…

A'LELIA WALKER (1885–1931): Heiress (to her mother C. J. Walker's beauty products empire), society queen, and arts matron. (She also helped bankroll this event.)

(Judging from photos, Hurston herself had been using Walker's mother's hair-straightening products since her Howard days—along with every other urban dwelling Black woman, it seems, which inspired Hurston's friend Richard Bruce Nugent to later sarcastically write: "where did all the *nappy haired* colored ladies go?")

LANGSTON HUGHES (1902–1967): Writer.

COUNTEE CULLEN (1903–1946): Poet.

In panels three and four we meet two other important figures in Hurston's life:

FANNIE HURST (1885–1968): Novelist, and…

ANNIE NATHAN MEYER (1867–1951): Writer, educator, and cofounder of Barnard College.

Hurston often ruffled other women's feathers with her penchant for grand entrances and other attention-stealing antics, and in this instance it was Paul Robeson's wife, Eslanda, who took umbrage. Sensing this, Hurston made a point of winning her over the next time they met—a gesture that soon became a regular part of Hurston's MO.

LEFT
*Hurston's Barnard benefactor: the hard-charging yet extremely complex Annie Nathan Meyer. A lifelong civil rights crusader, including women's rights, Nathan Meyer was also oddly opposed to voting rights for women—mainly because her hated sister, Maud Nathan, was a leading suffragist!*

PAGE 22
New York's Columbia University had been partially co-ed since the mid-1800s, yet women were still not allowed to enroll in their so-called "hard science" classes (let alone enter their postgraduate programs), ostensibly to prevent their tiny little brains from exploding. In a failed attempt to alter this policy, Annie Nathan Meyer spearheaded the creation of a "sister school" in 1889, eventually dubbed Barnard College, which was and remains essentially a branch of Columbia. Yet considering the progressive underpinnings justifying its creation, the fact that Hurston was Barnard's first non-white student—as late as 1925!—is astounding.

Nathan Meyer had long claimed—with sound justification—to be the sole founder of Barnard, yet for myriad political reasons (along with a big fat dose of old school Ivy League anti-Semitism), she still isn't officially recognized as a founder *at all.* Get on that, Barnard! Must you be late to the game with *everything?*

RIGHT
*The utterly fascinating Fannie Hurst.*

PAGE 23
While growing up as a pudgy, over-protected only child in a stuffy, upper middle-class, non-observant Jewish home in St., Louis, MO, a teenage Fannie Hurst vowed to make herself "fascinating"—and *boy* did she ever succeed. Moving to NYC after college graduation, she was soon a best-selling author, writing about her grueling six month experiences as a waitress/model/actress, the gist of which immediately became her formula: the struggling single girl, making it on her own against all odds. Initially winning critical praise, Hurst's name quickly became synonymous with *bad writing*—and deservedly so, considering her steadfast refusal to rewrite a single word of her hacked out novels. Even after her demise, comedic filmmakers like Woody Allen and Mel Brooks were using her name as a punch line. Yet thanks to her negotiating and promotional skills, this "Queen of the Weepers" was billed as the highest paid author of her era.

Hurst also epitomized the so-called "limousine liberal" that Hurston in particular grew to despise: showing up at fundraisers bedecked in diamonds and furs with air dogs in tow to guilt trip other rich white people into throwing more money at Black people's causes. "Negrotarians" was Hurston's term for such creatures. Oh, and while I'm busy making fun: Hurst's Fifth Avenue apartment (decorated in alleged Roman Catholic "relics" that even devout Roman Catholics paid too much for) had fifty-foot high ceilings. *FIFTY FOOT HIGH CEILINGS!* The woman was nothing if not a laughable caricature.

Yet Hurston *loved* Fannie Hurst. Not without reservations, of course, but how could she not love a fellow female author who reinvented herself from scratch and now had *everything*? She even had a husband (a Russian émigré pianist named Jacques S. Danielson) whom she tried to keep secret from the public lest her reputation as the spokeswoman for single working girls everywhere be ruined. Yet once her marital status was revealed, Hurst made sure to let the world know that she and her husband maintained *separate abodes* (which they in fact did), and this arrangement soon became euphemistically known as a "Fannie Hurst Marriage." This, to Hurston, sounded ideal (at least at the time), and was one of countless reasons why Hurst was (other than artistically) a role model for her.

Hurst and Hurston's friendship was peculiar from the start, in that the latter never stopped referring to the former as "*Miss* Fannie," and the former (who was raised by Black nannies in quasi-Southern Missouri) never bothered to correct her. Or that Hurston would pretend to have grown up dirt poor (which she most certainly hadn't), just to appease Hurst's assumptions (or to have a perverse laugh at her expense?), and which shed a bad light on *both* of them. And then there was Hurst's "Negro novel," *Imitation of Life* (which was twice made into a major motion picture during Hurston's lifetime), a book that Hurston secretly *hated*—what with its stock stereotypes of the Tragic Mulatto and the Long Suffering Mammy—yet one that Hurst credited her "pet Negro" with helping to inspire! And I'm just scratching the surface of their weirdness here. Yet they really were good, true friends to the bitter end. What can I say? Life is weird!

ABOVE
*The trendsetting Carl Van Vechten (with a friend).*

Equally remarkable—and equally ridiculous—was Carl Van Vechten, who was determined from the start to become Hurston's best friend—and actually succeeded! This Iowa native started his writing career as a classical music and dance critic for the *New York Times*, and was an early champion of modern dance. By the 1920s Van Vechten had become a fairly successful novelist as well, and was also renowned (some would say notorious) for his passion for Black artists, many of whom—Paul Robeson, Ethel Waters, Langston Hughes, etc.—he promoted aggressively.

Even though Van Vechten's homosexuality was an open secret, he had a long and happy marriage to the actress Fania Marinoff, who also shared his love for all things related to Black culture. In fact, their Upper East Side apartment was jokingly referred to as the "northern offices of the NAACP," due to the many mixed race parties and fundraisers they hosted there.

"Pet Negro" was Hurston's term to describe herself or any other Black person who played the role of any given white person's token Black friend. She later wrote an essay on this very subject, and not in a damning way either: she explained that, particularly in the South, such "pets" served as an important line of communication between the races, and it was a role she found herself playing countless times throughout her life.

RIGHT
*The absurdly literal cover image of the first edition of Van Vechten's controversial novel was sky blue, with the title and surrounding cloud embossed in gold.*

PAGE 25
Van Vechten was definitely courting controversy when he titled his book *Nigger Heaven* (a name that everyone—including his own father—tried in vain to dissuade him from using), but the pushback was more than he had bargained for when he found himself temporarily banned from his favorite haunts. Still, some Black writers, including Hurston and Langston Hughes, thought the book was an accurate portrayal of Harlem's nightlife, and were not shy about defending it in spite of its title.

Most of the bigger Harlem nightclubs such as the Cotton Club were white-owned and catered to a whites only clientele, while Harlem's locals patronized the neighborhood's many small, hidden speakeasies. Smalls Paradise was unique in that it was Black-owned, and welcomed customers of all races, so naturally it was Van Vechten's favorite destination.

DINGE QUEEN: A white man who is sexually attracted to Black men, and a term that described Van Vechten to a tee. In fact, many suspected that his passion for Black culture was just a ruse in order to disguise his true desires. Yet that would fail to explain his love of Hurston, both as an artist and a person, let alone the many other Black female artists he wrote about with such deep knowledge and enthusiasm that he couldn't *possibly* have been faking it.

ABOVE
*A 1932 tourist's map of Harlem.*

PAGE 26
Hurston moved constantly during her New York years, and even lived with Fannie Hurst in her palatial abode for a spell before relocating back to Harlem, where she felt far more at home. She also once shared an apartment with the writers and cousins Dorothy West and Helene Johnson, but most often roomed off and on with various members of a group of sexually ambiguous Black male writers who became her main posse during this time (and who jokingly referred to themselves as "the Niggerati," much to the consternation of their more self-conscious colleagues).

ABOVE
*A young Richard Bruce Nugent, along with a sample of his Beardsley-esque artwork.*

RICHARD BRUCE NUGENT (1906–1987), was the baby of the group, and was primarily a visual artist before focusing more on his poetry later in life. Lacking a work ethic, he tended to couch surf while earning spending money as a rent boy. He was also one of the very few men in that scene who was openly gay, though he was so brashly effeminate that there was little point in attempting to hide that fact.

Though Harlem attracted many gay men during its Renaissance heyday, there was still a deep stigma attached to being gay. Many of them could still hear their mothers saying, "You already have one cross to bear. Why take on another?"—the implication also being that it was a *choice*, and which resulted in many of them attempting to "cure" themselves via marriage, usually with disastrous results (even Nugent vainly attempted the "marriage cure" many years later).

Such was not the case with gay women at the time, however, since lesbianism and female bisexuality were not only accepted but were even something of a fad, and popular performers such as Ma Rainey and Moms Mabley even incorporated their sexual preferences into their acts. Meanwhile, Ethel Waters (by then already a huge star) used to get into such loud, public shouting matches with her girlfriends *du jour* that fellow lesbian blues singer Alberta Hunter declared her "an embarrassment to the tribe."

Even though Nugent once described Hurston as a "try anything once" kind of a gal, she was also very discreet, and may well have written that hilarious double entendre in her diary simply to titillate her nosy roommate. Besides, Hurston was always quite specific when it came to her own sexual preferences: she liked young, solidly built Black men—"wrasslin' men," she called them—though preferably ones with at least some education, so that they'd have something to talk about once the "wrasslin'" was over with. (And although Hurston had been courted by many white men in her life, the interest wasn't mutual, with her explaining simply that she didn't feel comfortable "getting naked" with them.)

Nugent outlived most of his Renaissance colleagues by decades, and thus became the go-to source for anyone researching that time in history. Fortunately for Hurston, he only had the fondest memories of her, and even described her as being the "living embodiment" of the Renaissance movement.

The "fiancé" mentioned on this page is Herbert Sheen, though he and Hurston were still as unserious about marriage as ever, and had long practiced a formally agreed-to open relationship.

PAGE 27
On this page, I used stuffy old Alain Locke as a stand-in for the many Black intellectuals who desperately distanced themselves from any and all stereotypically "Negro" trappings that white racists were inclined to ridicule.

Locke wasn't the only one who was critical of Hurston's lack of literary output during this time. Her own best friends also muttered about it (though most likely behind her back), wishing she'd simply write down the many remembrances and folktales she'd share "for free" at parties. But aside from socializing, school (and later, field research) came first, and it would be years before she started writing in earnest again.

LEFT
*This is one of only two known photos of Wallace Thurman (and he appeared to be in his teens in the other one).*

WALLACE THURMAN (1902–1934), the latest member of Hurston's "Niggerati" inner circle, was raised in a whorehouse in Salt Lake City, UT, of all places. A sickly child with a genius IQ who barely made it into adulthood, he bounced around the West Coast before winding up in New York, working as an editor for the socialist-leaning Black newspaper *The Messenger* (not that he believed in socialism—in fact, Thurman could probably be described as a *nihilist*). This deeply troubled man struggled with his homosexuality and ultra-dark skin. ("How dare he be so dark!" Nugent thought when he first met him.) He died at the age of thirty-two from tuberculosis, which was exacerbated by his chronic alcoholism.

Thurman is best-known for his first novel, *The Blacker the Berry*, which deals with the intraracial politics surrounding skin color, though I'd also highly recommend his second novel, *Infants of the Spring*—a relentlessly cynical fictionalized memoir of Thurman's Harlem Renaissance days, in which none of his former peers are spared from his withering descriptions. (His barely disguised Hurston stand-in portrayed her as being little more than a grifter!) Thurman was highly critical of their movement's achievements in general, declaring that none of them had produced anything worthy of posterity. (Interestingly, Hurston herself rarely spoke of the movement in later years, and in her autobiography referred to it only once, and as the "*so-called* Harlem Renaissance" movement. Yet her correspondences reveal that she maintained a warm, fraternal bond with many of its participants for years afterward.)

Both Nugent and Thurman used to cover their walls with homoerotic murals (their subjects were almost always Caucasian—a shared preference, apparently), though it's unlikely these images graced the walls while Hurston was living with them.

RIGHT
*Aaron Douglas's* FIRE!! *cover was mostly a solid black, with a deep red added for color. Douglas was also quite busy doing covers for* FIRE!!*'s hated competition (though I'm guessing* The Messenger *couldn't afford him).*

PAGE 28 AND 29
Though this core group—Hurston, Hughes, Thurman, and Nugent—were the driving forces behind the single issue of *FIRE!! Devoted to Younger Negro Artists*, the magazine included contributions from many of their young peers, including Gwendolyn Bennett, Countee Cullen, Arna Bontemps, and Helene Johnson, as well as interior and cover art by Aaron Douglas, who's best remembered today for his stunning murals. (I should note here that I shamelessly mimicked Douglas's lettering style for the cover of this book.)

Hurston contributed two pieces to *FIRE!!*: her award-winning play *Color Struck* and a short story, "Sweat," which would be her last published work of fiction until 1933.

*FIRE!!*'s contributors noted with pride that they were all under the age of thirty. Only Hurston knew that she was in fact thirty-five years old at the time.

Getting "banned in Boston" was ridiculously easy to do back when that city was ruled by the Catholic version of the Taliban, which tended to encourage publishers and distributors to let the rest of the world know when any of their books or films achieved such a status, assuming it would arouse people's prurient interests.

PAGE 30
Nugent's sole contribution to *FIRE!!*, a story called "Smoke, Lilies and Jade," was a surprising high point in the magazine. Written in a stream of consciousness, paragraph-free style, with "sentences" separated only by ellipses, Nugent's thoughts meander from his current living situation to the circumstances surrounding his leaving his middle-class family's home for good, all told with a real-time, mood-shifting honesty. Most readers *hated* it, not surprisingly, and I can't help but wonder what his own cohorts made of it, since there's no record of their thoughts on it.

With rare exceptions, neither Hurston nor the rest of her closest colleagues' work—Hughes and Wallace in particular—were well received by the Black press during this time, due perhaps to their defying Du Bois and Locke's propagandist agenda, or simply out of fear that their unvarnished tales would scandalize their skittish advertisers. The smug, prudish editors of *Baltimore Afro-American* in particular will prove to have a long history of treating Hurston so poorly that she would have been well justified in burning their offices down to the ground!

Hurston's baby brother, Everett, at one point looked to be the lone ne'er-do-well in the Hurston clan, as he bounced from one sibling's sofa to the next, wearing out his welcome all the while. But eventually he applied for a job as a mailman in Brooklyn, NY, and stayed with that job until his retirement. He also wound up supplementing his income by investing in rental property.

ABOVE
*Professor "Papa" Franz Boas, posing for a diorama in 1895.*

PAGE 31 AND 32
The German born DR. FRANZ BOAS (1858–1942) was by this point America's premier anthropologist. He also mentored the next generation of brilliant anthropologists including Ruth Benedict and Melville Herskovits, both of whom, along with Boas, mentored Hurston as well. (Meanwhile, the soon-to-be world famous Margaret Mead was one of Hurston's classmates.) Boas was a proponent of the theory of cultural relativism, which argued that there's no point in claiming that one culture is "better" or "superior" to another, since each culture exists for an explicit purpose: its people's survival. This theory helped to confirm Hurston's growing sense that there was nothing "second rate" about African-American culture, and it instilled in her a determination to both study it *and* celebrate it.

Boas also was an ideal role model for Hurston at this time; he was cold and analytical in his approach to his research on the one hand, yet also remained a warm, generous—and even *silly*—human being on the other. For his part, Boas openly worried that Hurston's artistic nature would be in constant conflict with her scientific aspirations, and he also correctly assumed that "Artist Zora" would win out in the end. Boas taught at Columbia, which is why Hurston is suddenly pictured with male classmates.

As mentioned earlier, Barnard was and is affiliated with Columbia, so students are (and were) free to enroll in classes at both schools.

RIGHT
*For practical reasons, Hurston usually dressed in white from head to toe while crisscrossing the hot South on her many field trips. I chose to dress her in light yellow for the purposes of this book, however, in order to give her a color "signifier." (It's a comic book thing, you wouldn't understand.)*

PAGE 33 AND 34
In order to fully subsidize her field trip, Hurston took on a bit more than she could handle in the form of modest-paying side projects. One was at the behest of historian DR. CARTER WOODSON (1875–1950), widely regarded as the father of Black history, and the creator of the still-running Association for the Study of Negro Life and History. The thorough-minded Woodson offered a modest fee to any Black scholar visiting the South in return for them digging up any and all courthouse records of Black-related churches and businesses. (Langston Hughes was performing this same grueling task in Mobile, AL, at the very same time that Hurston was in Jacksonville.)

Hurston was also hired by Annie Nathan Meyer to write a novelized version of the latter's controversial play, *Black Souls* (the message of which was to highlight the passive—yet damning—role white women played in the then-epidemic lynching of Black men, most of which were based on unproven sexual allegations designed to cover up their own transgressions). This collaboration hit a curious roadblock when Hurston objected to the way the play's female lead, the spoiled daughter of a Southern Senator, aggressively pursued the Black male lead—basically by insisting that such a scenario could never happen. Nathan Meyer insisted that such scenarios could and *did* happen, but Hurston wouldn't budge. We can only speculate as to whether Hurston was sure of her own assumption, or was simply concocting an excuse to extract herself from that time-consuming job. Hurston's honeymoon was hardly the first time she'd slept with Sheen, so the lack of "fireworks" could only have been her response to the claustrophobia and/or entrapment that she associated with marriage—or any exclusive sexual relationship, for that matter. She and Sheen tried to make the marriage work for several years by employing the Fannie Hurst-style arrangement. Yet while Hurst and her husband lived mere blocks apart from each other, Sheen's medical practice was based in Chicago (and later, St. Louis), while the technically New York-based Hurston spent their short-lived marriage traveling to just about everywhere but Chicago or St. Louis! So it was just a matter of time before they both threw in the towel.

Hurston often expressed an understandable longing for an ideal man that she could share her life with—one that would encourage and support her career, specifically—and then despair of any such man even existing. Out of sympathy, her biographers seem more than willing to attribute this failure to the prevailing chauvinistic attitudes held by the Black men of her era. Leaving aside the blatant bigotry built into that assumption, I couldn't find any evidence to suggest that Herbert Sheen *wasn't* that man, since during their short marriage she lived her life unencumbered by any expectations on his part. I also can't find any evidence of her making any efforts or compromises on *his* behalf (like, say, visiting *him* even once). And when they were together, any offer or invite she received would send her flying out the door, all the while resenting any questions being asked of her as to where or why or *when will you be back*—a pattern that persisted throughout all of her future relationships.

I don't mean to sound overly critical of Hurston regarding her relationship woes, but when in the throes of her more self-pitying moments she was a little too inclined to overlook her own contributions to her situation—particularly her general unwillingness to make any compromises herself. Besides, the most important component to any successful relationship is to simply physically *be there*, and that was one thing that the restless and conflict-averse Hurston totally sucked at.

Sheen would later joke that Hurston's divorcing him was the worst thing that ever happened to him—because his second wife was a total bitch (*ba-doom tish*)! And as previously mentioned, they remained close friends, and in her later years, Hurston wasn't the least bit shy about occasionally hitting him up for a "loan," to which he regularly obliged. Yet it's telling that Hurston never once commented on the fact that she walked away from being a *doctor's wife*—not a bad gig for anyone's ledger—let alone expressed a moment's regret over it, all of which goes to show how independent she truly was.

ABOVE
*(L) Langston Hughes in the mid-1920s. (R) Hurston used to read passages from Hughes's second collection of poetry (with a title that was almost as controversial as* Nigger Heaven*) to Black Southerners she'd befriend, and her listeners would then improvise songs based on the poems. Soon they were insisting that Hurston read the book at parties, and began referring to it as "the party book."*

PAGE 35
Midwestern native Langston Hughes once recalled a speech he gave at his high school graduation, in which he declared both his fellow graduates and the faculty sitting before him to be the finest group of scholars ever to be assembled in one place. "The speech was well received," he reported wryly. I recount this story since it perfectly illustrates the biggest difference between Hughes and Hurston, both as writers and as people.

From the moment they first met, both Hurston and Hughes shared a love and fascination for all aspects of African-American life, and both were equally determined to express that love in their art—even in the face of tremendous pressure to edit those sentiments, along with condemnation for their refusal to do so. Yet while Hurston was never reluctant to tell the world to go to hell, Langston was, particularly on a personal level, an incurable people-pleaser (the result, most likely, of being born to an immature, narcissistic mother and a self-hating, impossible-to-please father—though we'd best not delve *too* deeply into Hughes's complicated upbringing here). This crowd-pleasing tendency inevitably seeped into Hughes's work, resulting in him fluctuating between sounding like a coolly defiant iconoclast to an anthem-composing racial cheerleader, with the latter becoming more prominent as he got older (and why it's rare to stumble upon an African-American arts-related book or website that *doesn't* open with a quote from one of Hughes's poems). Still, there is no denying Hughes's formidable talent, and Hurston herself had long admired his skillful use of the English language. Yet it wasn't until the two of them stumbled into each other in Mobile—and subsequently spent a lot of time together on the road—that the two of them became uniquely close.

"The Negro farthest down" was Hurston's term to describe a poor, humble, uneducated Black person, and was in no way meant to be derogatory.

LEFT
*"Godmother."*

PAGE 36
CHARLOTTE LOUISE VAN DER VEER QUICK OSGOOD MASON (1854–1946) was descended from the oldest of "old money," to which her Knickerbocker father compounded with "new" money by becoming a railroad tycoon. She later married an egomaniacal quack named Dr. Rufus Osgood Mason, who incorporated alleged "traditional native healing practices" into his own medical practice, and developed a huge cult-like following as a result. No one believed in her husband more than Charlotte herself, and after he passed away she seemed to embody his love of the "primitive" as well as his all-consuming persona. The childless Mason soon had accumulated a cult of her own (consisting mostly of adoring, well-bred young women), and also began anonymously subsidizing detailed research in Native American culture, resulting most famously in Natalie Curtis's massive 1907 tome, *The Indians' Book* (which Mason practically cowrote—anonymously, of course).

By the 1920s, Mason, along with many other wealthy white people, had caught the "Negro bug," and was soon looking for ways to subsidize research into African-American culture—particularly if it led to establishing links with the African continent ("African Roots" by this time had become an obsession with her). Not surprisingly, Mason's sudden arrival in the Harlem arts scene inspired mixed responses—the optics alone were the source of much hilarity—with some people, most notably Paul Robeson, finding her "repulsive." Yet others, particularly Alain Locke, couldn't help but notice that her interest in her new favorite subject was sincere, and that her knowledge was deep (plus she had those deep, deep pockets). So he introduced her to Langston Hughes, who quickly became her well-funded protégé, and who in turn introduced Mason to Hurston.

PAGE 37 AND 38
"Big Sweet" left such a lasting impression on Hurston that she became something of a stock character in a few of her future (and mostly unfinished) plays.

This story serves as a reminder—as it must have to Hurston herself—that her fieldwork included some very real health risks!

PAGE 39 AND 40
Hurston's initial curiosity in the world of voodoo (or "hoodoo," which was the term Hurston ascribed to its practice in New Orleans, while reserving the term "voodoo" for its Haitian variations) soon became an obsession, and led to her researching and writing about it extensively. It is also a complex, varied, and ever-evolving world—and Hurston herself was the first to admit that she'd barely scratched the surface on the topic—which is why some researchers who followed in her footsteps found much to criticize in her own research.

Still, most of what was written on the subject *before* Hurston came along was written by white men, who couldn't possibly have immersed themselves into that world to the extent that she did. Voodoo's believers and patrons were, first and foremost, Black women—who, being the least likely to find justice in the court of law, would turn to "two-headed doctors" to seek justice (or vengeance, take your pick).

The legend of voodoo priestess MARIE LAVEAU (1794–1881), as well as that of her daughter, MARIE LAVEAU II (1827–1895) still looms large in New Orleans, and even more so back when Hurston was studying up on the subject.

LEFT
*An old painting based on another old painting of Marie Laveau I.*

PAGE 41
Apologies to cat lovers everywhere! Yet before you hurl this book into the fire in disgust, keep in mind that this initiation rite was clearly designed to separate the wheat from the chaff—the "true believers" from the mere "dabblers." Hurston was an animal lover herself, but she was also surely imagining what Dr. Boas would say if she had wimped out right after she had gotten her foot in the door.

PAGE 42
This story clearly illustrates voodoo's power of suggestion—which, indeed, is what its power is totally reliant on. That plus its practitioners' unquestioning faith in its powers, which in turn can make even a skeptic pause (as in the case of the "victim" shown here).

Interestingly, Hurston tells this story (which, like the previous voodoo tales, originally appeared in her first folktale collection, *Mules and Men*) unquestioningly, as if she herself had no doubt that voodoo's powers are real. Yet if that were truly the case, she'd also be admitting to taking part in an *attempted murder* plot here, rather than simply helping to con a wronged woman out of her money—*twice* (though the woman did ultimately get what she wanted, so…money well spent!). Thus, I took the liberty of adding the final "what a racket" thought balloon here. If that makes me a spoilsport then so be it, but I'm not going to let Hurston con *me* as well!

PAGE 43 AND 44
Hurston always insisted that while she loved Langston Hughes, she wasn't *in love* with him, but her behavior sure told another story. The problem was that Hughes was gay—or "celibate," according to him, since he was so deeply buried in the closet that he must have reeked of mothballs—so she had to sublimate her romantic feelings for him by awkwardly recasting him as a creative partner. Anything to keep them connected, basically—and to her credit, she at least never attempted to "cure" him of his homosexuality, like so many of her female friends attempted to do with their many gay male acquaintances. Indeed, she seemed to understand and respect Hughes's sexuality more than he himself did.

Ah, but Hughes was also a handsome, charming, intelligent, and talented man, and thus the object of many people's affections (and frustrations), so it's no wonder that Hurston's alarm bells went off when another woman—a *pretty* one at that, and with a *history* of attempting "cures"—intruded on their cozy little scene (and make no mistake: Hurston was as big a "fag hag" as there ever was, so she could suss the likes of Thompson from a mile away). Making matters worse was Hughes's habit of placating people, especially women (hello, mommy issues!), so it's no wonder that it all devolved into a hot, smoldering mess.

LOUISE THOMPSON PATTERSON (1901–1999) was more invested in the political activities of the Harlem Renaissance movement than in its artistic and literary aspects, and she later married William L. Patterson, a prominent (and leading Black) member of the American Communist party. Thompson was most likely sent by "Godmother" Mason to spy on Hurston and Hughes as much as to assist them, only in this instance Mason—an otherwise master triangulator—inadvertently created a triangle that was out of her control.

LEFT
*Louise Thompson and Langston Hughes en route to the USSR, 1932. No "curing" going on here, no sir!*

PAGE 45
Karamu House (originally called The Playhouse Settlement) was started by RUSSELL AND ROWENA JELIFFE (pictured here with Hughes) as an ethnically diverse arts community, but quickly evolved into the country's premier center of African-American theater. Langston Hughes in particular had a long working history with the theater. (The original theater—which I could not find a picture of—burned down

in 1938, so I just took a wild guess here at how it may have looked.)

Many letters between Hurston and Hughes crossed paths during the intervening year, with one party receiving a reconciliatory note while the other received one chock-full of recriminations, to which each party responded in kind. Soon Hurston was threatening lawsuits, while Hughes wound up crying uncle…and then *this*. A classic tale of a woman scorned, only in this case no romance was ever involved.

"Godmother" Mason had cut off Hughes's financial support unexpectedly, and for the vaguest of reasons—a "lack of sincere interest in Mother Africa" or some such nonsense, leaving him emotionally and financially devastated. (Unlike Mason, Hughes had actually *been* to Africa while working as a merchant marine, and was not impressed with what he saw there.) This was during the depths of the Depression, after all, and he suddenly found himself desperately scrambling. This turn of events certainly alarmed Hurston, who was inclined to blame Alain Locke's machinations for Hughes's predicament, though Mason's own troubled finances were the real issue (she took a huge hit from the stock market crash herself, and was desperate to find ways to cut corners). Still, why she cut off Hughes and *not* Hurston is hard to decipher.

PAGE 46

A modern reader is sure to wonder why Hurston didn't punch "Godmother" in the nose at this point. The reasons as to why she didn't are: one, she was still reliant on her money. Two, Hurston at this point was so deeply invested in her still-new "Black pride" mindset that she would occasionally fall into the trap of castigating white people to make her case. And Mason would join in with her at these moments, commenting on how Caucasians lacked "soul"; that they're "lost in the machine" and thus are "too detached from nature," etc. (excluding herself, of course). So for Hurston to suddenly take offense at any negative generalizations made about her *own* kind would have, at least at that moment, sounded hypocritical.

And three, Hurston truly loved Mason, and in a way that made her relationship with Fannie Hurst seem *normal* in comparison. Some speculate that Hurston still craved a maternal figure—a role that Mason was more than willing and eager to fill—though she already knew other older women who could—and had—filled that role, and… well, she really was *too old* to be looking for that in anybody by that point. Finally: could Hurston have actually drank the Kool-Aid and *become* a member of the Mason cult? Well, no, not really, since she was never *blind* to the old gal's many faults. Instead, Hurston may simply have appreciated Mason's wisdom and (usually) sage advice, and been truly grateful for her generous five-plus years of patronage, as well she should have been.

By this time Van Vechten had inherited a fortune from a deceased relative, and was no longer obliged to write for a living. Instead he focused on his hobby of portrait photography, which soon led to a second career, and for which he is today best remembered. In fact, his portraits of his countless artist friends still adorn many a book's dust jacket, including Hurston's.

ABOVE

*Hurston looking "fierce," in one of countless photos taken of her by Van Vechten.*

Hurston was at least partially correct regarding the trip to Russia that Hughes et al. had undertaken. Thompson was the only "true believer" in the crew—most involved had no idea what communism even *meant*—and one blunder after another left them all scattered and scrambling to get back home. Hughes himself remained behind for an extended stay, however, and wrote and published many positive things about the People's Revolution (no doubt partially to appease his hosts)—while simultaneously denouncing

America—as he traveled deep into the USSR's interior. Not surprisingly, Hughes wound up spending a lot of time and effort attempting to walk back from these words over the next two decades.

Van Vechten tried for years to arrange a reconciliation between Hughes and Hurston, to no avail. Hurston was too prideful—and too *embarrassed*—to ever contact Hughes again, while Hughes most likely never got over his anger at her, though he was way too passive to ever say as much. Instead, he summed up their relationship in his own autobiography with a dismissive "Girls are funny creatures." What a doofus.

PAGE 47

This show was the first of many attempts by Hurston to write and/or stage her own theatrical productions, yet most never got past the planning stage—and the few that did, while well received, were hardly a financial success. The main problem, as with her past entrepreneurial attempts, was that she was never very good at handling money, nor was she comfortable in the role of "boss." Yet she also felt that much of what she'd seen and heard in her fieldwork could *only* be conveyed on the stage, as opposed to the written word, and so she kept trying.

Still, Mason and Locke weren't wrong about the theater being an unwelcome distraction for her. Hurston still had yet to establish herself as a writer, and it was past time for her to start prioritizing.

PAGE 48

A hurricane hit the Bahamas while Hurston was visiting there (she vividly recalled hanging onto a palm tree for dear life), which destroyed Nassau's infrastructure. Hurston suffered from gastric pain off and on for the rest of her life, which she attributed to the ensuing unsanitary living conditions she was forced to endure. Yet her health woes (which she never gave a name to, nor did she ever identify the meds she was taking) remained so persistent that it couldn't have been from food poisoning or a parasitic infection. More likely it was something chronic, such as colitis.

Hurston never mastered the typewriter, and wrote everything out in longhand. Sadly, this also entailed finding and paying someone to transcribe her work before she could submit it. Fortunately for her, she found someone in Sanford who typed out her entire first novel for only $2.

After a long drought, Hurston published a doozy of a short story in 1933 called "The Gilded Six-Bits," about a woman who was so turned on by playing a sex-for-money game with her husband that she wound up having sex for money for real with another man. Yet rather than having her marriage or reputation destroyed, she simply had to endure being in the dog house until her husband overcame his anger, after which they resumed playing "make-believe prostitute." It was *The Scarlet Letter* turned on its head, and was so deftly written that readers were *charmed* rather than scandalized by its blatant perversity. It was also what brought Hurston to the attention of publisher Bertram Lippincott.

Hurston had a lot of extended family in Sanford, just down the road from Eatonville. The small house she was staying in at this time once belonged to her uncle, and it's still standing as I write this, in all of its un-remodeled glory.

PAGE 49

Hurston's first novel, *Jonah's Gourd Vine*, was generally well received, and sold better than expected (though in those days sales expectations for Black authors weren't very high, since their potential market was perceived to be much lower). Pictured in panel one is *New York Times Book Review* critic Margaret Wallace (an open lesbian, yet also a prolific author of steamy heterosexual romance novels), who totally nailed it on the head in her glowing review of the book. Yet Hurston was more angrily fixated on the review of yet another *Times* critic, John Chamberlain (shown in panel two, and later to become a founding editor of the libertarian-leaning *The Freeman*). Though he liked the book, Chamberlain could not have been more demonstratively wrong in his naïve assessment of Black preachers' poetic gifts (or lack thereof), since the climactic speech he cited here was actually a verbatim transcription of a sermon Hurston recorded by a Florida-based preacher named C. C. Lovelace.

Panels three and four are an amalgam of the usual bellyaching that Hurston long had to endure from the bulk of the Black press—Du Bois's *The Crisis* in particular. Before Hurston, no writer had even attempted to capture, let alone *master*, a specific Southern Black dialect to such great effect, yet these reviewers reacted to it with an indignant, exasperated "here we go again." Like, *HUH?!?*

Many Northerners of both races were unaware that all-Black towns existed in the South—and apparently *refused* to believe it even after being informed of that fact.

Considering the ambivalent feelings she had toward the man, Hurston did a remarkable job of getting into her father's head in this book (which, though technically about both of her parents, is mostly about him), and this surprisingly sympathetic portrayal surely must have served as a "healing process" for her (if you'll pardon my use of that nauseating contemporary term). And as is typical of Hurston, the dialogue is often quite hilarious, and even downright *saucy*—such as when, upon noticing the effect his son has on women, John's white biological father declares him to be a "walking orgasm"!

ABOVE
*The incredibly talented Mexican artist Miguel Covarrubias illustrated Hurston's first folklore collection, 1935's* Mules and Men. *During Covarrubias's New York years (1925–1930), he was a fixture in Harlem's nightclub scene, and drew many brilliant caricatures of that world's participants.*

PAGE 50
KATHERINE DUNHAM (1909–2006) was a dancer, choreographer, anthropologist, and the leader of her own successful dance troupe, which specialized in incorporating dances from throughout the African Diaspora. This page is based on a passage from Dunham's own autobiography (and later recounted in Valerie Boyd's Hurston bio), in which she reveals the competitiveness she felt upon meeting Hurston for the first time in a hilariously self-deprecating manner.

Dunham wound up getting on Hurston's nerves shortly after this, when the latter was on her first (and she hoped, groundbreaking) folklore-hunting trip to Jamaica, only to discover that Dunham had beaten her to every village she visited only weeks before! Hurston had to remind herself that Dunham was there to collect music and dance, rather than folklore, in order to remain placated.

MELVILLE HERSKOVITS (1895–1963), awkwardly dubbed "the Jewish father of African-American studies," actually wound up supervising Hurston during her Harlem head-measuring expedition.

RIGHT
*Katherine Dunham in 1943. You can see much of her Hollywood cameo work on YouTube.*

PAGE 51
Hurston won a Guggenheim grant in 1935 in order to fund a field trip to the Caribbean, only it came with the strange caveat that she also had to return to Columbia and earn a master's degree. The problem was, she didn't want a master's degree, yet when she informed the foundation (as well as the Columbia administration, who now were butting in) of that fact, they responded by spitefully cutting her grant money in half—while *still* insisting she attend grad school! So Hurston responded in kind, by living off of the money and skipping class entirely. Eventually cooler heads prevailed and grad school was dropped from the discussion, but she still wound up heading to Jamaica with far less money than she had originally been promised.

New York City native PERCIVAL PUNTER (1912–1985) sang in yet another of Hurston's short-lived musicals, 1932's *The Great Day*. Their courtship started a bit slower than I made it appear here. They had to circle around each other a few times first.

LEFT
*Percival Punter.*

PAGE 52
Describing him as "the great love" of her life, Hurston and Punter had an intense, stormy, on-again, off-again relationship for roughly eight years. They adored each other, yet they were also doomed from the start—primarily due to the fact that he was twenty-one years younger than her, and behaved the way all young lovers do: with a constant need of reassurance and attention. It also didn't help that Hurston was

by now a rising literary star (her first folklore collection, *Mules and Men*, was also in print by now, to generally good sales and reviews), and was being feted accordingly by everyone everywhere, making Punter feel invisible whenever he accompanied her. (Hurston would in turn become jealous when younger women were around him, when she otherwise was not the jealous type at all.)

Hurston informed numerous friends that she wrote *Their Eyes Were Watching God* while in Haiti in an attempt to purge herself of the intense feelings she still had for Punter—yet this came as news to Punter when he was informed of it decades later by Hurston's first biographer, Robert Hemenway, replying that he "didn't see any tears" as she walked out the door and onto a southbound train.

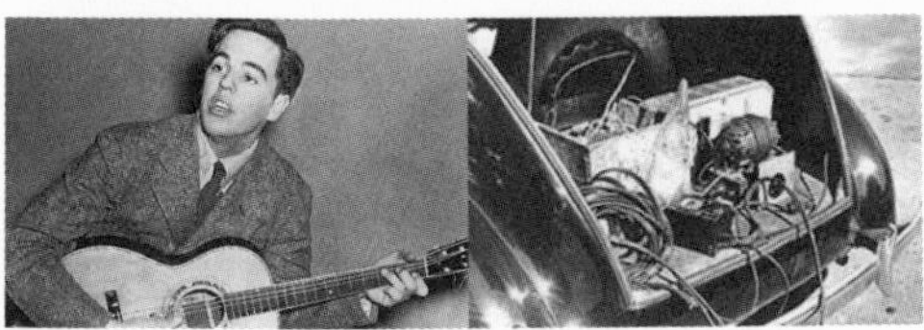

ABOVE
*(L) Alan Lomax, and (R) his cumbersome yet "state of the art" portable recording equipment, circa 1936. Many of the backwoods communities he and Hurston visited still had no electricity, so the equipment had to be powered by his car's battery.*

PAGE 53 AND 54
Before heading to the Caribbean, Hurston made another folklore-collecting trip, this time accompanied by the young ALAN LOMAX (1915–2002), son of the legendary folklorist (and hero to Hurston) John A. Lomax. This and a few of Hurston's subsequent folklore gathering trips were funded by the Federal Government's massive new Works Progress Administration (or WPA), the formation of which Hurston had philosophical reservations about—yet due to the Great Depression's prolonged nature, the private funding that she'd previously enjoyed had all but dried up. Thus, if she wished to continue with her fieldwork—which she did—she often had little choice but to work with the Feds.

Page 53 recounts a story that Lomax later shared, which occurred while he and Hurston were recording music and stories in and around South Carolina's Gullah Islands. Taking an immediate liking to the young Lomax, Hurston no doubt enjoyed showing off her ability to "flip" from "Harvard to Harlem" (or, more specifically, from "Barnardese" to "Eatonvilleese") on a dime. Yet her occasional casual use of the n-word—even in the presence of a white man—stands in sharp contrast to the way she reacted to a mixed race situation on the very next page.

RIGHT
*Mary Barnicle (photographed by Lomax).*

MARY ELIZABETH BARNICLE CADLE (1891–1978) was an English professor at NYU, a civil rights activist, and a folklorist, as well as a long-time collaborator with the senior Lomax. Not much information is available about her online, while the only *negative* comments one can find about her all came from Hurston, who couldn't stand her. For one thing, she epitomized (in Hurston's eyes) the white Northern liberal do-gooder, a "type" that she was increasingly growing to resent. Yet her stated reasons (as spelled out in her unintentionally hilarious tattletale letters to John Lomax) tended to consist of such "crimes" as her far-left politics, and her (alleged) excessive drinking. And exacerbating all of this was the maternal—and rather possessive—behavior both of these childless women exhibited toward young Alan (in fact, both women were actively recruiting him to take part in their own future projects behind the other's back), and it in many ways mirrored Hurston's earlier unhealthy triangle with Langston Hughes and Louise Thompson.

Still, it's interesting to see how even a defiantly *un*-politically correct iconoclast like Hurston could still be "triggered" (using today's parlance) by what someone could choose—or not choose—to interpret as a clear sign of racism. It *does* all come down to context, though much of the context here could simply be boiled down to "I *hate* you, lady."

PAGE 55
The information here (as well as pages 56 and 57) is cribbed from Hurston's second folklore collection, *Tell My Horse*, which

covers the folklore she unearthed (along with many social and political observations) while in Jamaica and, later, in Haiti.

Alice Walker once alleged that publishers used to *under*-edit Black authors' books, figuring that their presumed lower sales didn't warrant the extra time and resources on their part. If true, that surely would have explained the bumpy jumble that is *Tell My Horse*, where a strong editorial hand would have come in handy. The book lacks an overall context, for starters, and a simple third-person introduction explaining the book's purpose would have been most helpful. And Hurston bit off way more than she—or anyone—could chew here, subject matter-wise, in that it could have easily been broken into *three* books, which is what it in fact is.

In the Jamaica section of *Horse*, Hurston lovingly details the rites and practices of the island's remote interior inhabitants, yet her criticism of society in the capital of Kingston is quite damning, particularly regarding the treatment of women, which shocked and disgusted her (conversely, Hurston's Jamaican-born poet friend, Countee Cullen, expressed an equal amount of shock and disgust over how rigidly the South's Jim Crow laws were enforced when he first came to America).

PAGE 56
Hurston wrote *Their Eyes Were Watching God* in fifty-six days, and the version that wound up in print is, for the most part, a first draft (Lippincott, to his credit, said he wouldn't dare *touch* such a singular piece of work). In comparison to the amount of labor she put into the problematic *Tell My Horse*, it's telling how effortlessly she managed to bang out her undisputed masterpiece. But then the novel is really all about herself, in the way that it paralleled her own life up to that point. The only major difference between Hurston and her fictional stand-in, Janie Crawford, is how Janie's story revolved much more around the men in her life, albeit with each man serving as a milestone, measuring the slow evolution in her own self-regard and self-confidence. Yet not unlike Hurston, she winds up alone, and without any sense of financial security, yet perfectly content to be that way—the message being: "whatever life throws at me now, I know I can take it."

LEFT
*Hurston's "zombie," whose real name was Felicia Felix-Mentor.*

PAGE 57
While promoting *Tell My Horse*, the most common question Hurston was asked was "are zombies *real?!?*" The accurate answer to this would be "who really knows," though she certainly relished discussing its logistical and pharmacological possibilities. Still, the odds of the victim first surviving being paralyzed (most likely by using poison from a toad or a puffer fish), then buried alive for several days, and then later revived with the use of hallucinogens—and all without the perpetrator getting caught—is quite miniscule. The more likely—though less exotic—explanation would be that the victim was simply captured, and then regularly beaten and drugged to cause disorientation and wear down resistance, and then sold into slavery. (The woman Hurston met here most likely outlived her master's usefulness, and was thus "freed.")

A "bocor," according to Hurston, is a Haitian voodoo priest who specializes in the dark arts, and who has no moral reservations. Hurston of course "knew" that her gastric pain was simply her chronic condition flaring up (and possibly exacerbated by a mild case of malaria she contracted while there), but she couldn't help but worry that a bocor was shadowing her!

PAGE 58
The family-run J. B. Lippincott Publishing company was founded in 1836, and for many years was one of the biggest book publishers in the world. They published six books in all by Hurston between 1934 and 1942: three novels, two collections of folklore, and an autobiography. Hurston had a friendly and mutually beneficial relationship with her editor, Bertram Lippincott, even though none of her books were a "breakthrough" hit. So by the mid-1940s she decided she ought to try her hand with another outfit, and Lippincott didn't object too strenuously.

The novel Hurston mentions here was called *Moses, Man of the Mountain*, and was published in 1939. This odd yet ambitious tale is a retelling of the Old Testament's *Book of Exodus*, a story that resounded powerfully with African-Americans (particularly those who remembered the days of slavery), and one that Hurston had certainly heard, discussed, and related to many times in her youth. Thus, Hurston reimagines it here recast as a specifically Black American story (though she keeps the original geography intact), and it's fascinating to see how Moses goes from speaking the King's English (naturally, since he was part of the Pharaoh's court) only to slowly evolve into an unmistakably Southern Black accent, as he proceeds to lead his "people" out of slavery.

Partly due to its ambitious nature, *Moses* can be a bit of a bumpy read at times, but it's a fascinating read as well, in that it manages to make several major points simultaneously (and, as always, it is often quite hilarious). It also is the *favorite* book of many hardcore Hurston fans.

I couldn't find a single photo of Bertram Lippincott or his brother, so I simply faked it here.

LEFT
*Stetson Kennedy: Man Undercover! Kennedy's Klan exposés were originally too hot to handle for US publishers, and instead were first published in France in 1954 by the philosopher Jean-Paul Sartre.*

PAGE 59
STETSON KENNEDY (1916–2011) was a crusading (and, some claimed, self-aggrandizing) journalist and activist, best remembered for infiltrating the Ku Klux Klan in the 1940s, which led to a best-selling exposé. Both he and Hurston worked together briefly out of the Jacksonville, FL, offices of the WPA, though unlike Kennedy, she was denied her own workspace there (and even had to enter and exit through the back door), so it was no surprise that the WPA also made the inexperienced, twenty-three year old Kennedy her "supervisor."

Mixed race couples were also forbidden to travel together in the Jim Crow South, even if there was a twenty-five year age gap between them and the travel was work-related, so they'd have to arrive at destinations at different times and in separate cars. (Hurston was also frequently stopped and questioned while traveling with Alan Lomax, in spite of the fact that Mary Barnacle—an older white woman—was also traveling with them.)

Prior to WWII, there were many "company towns" in the US where the employers would take advantage of their remoteness by paying the employees in "scrip," which was redeemable only at the overpriced company store, thus leaving the employees in debt and held in virtual serfdom. But the brutal nature of the camp Hurston stumbled upon here was more akin to actual slavery. Both Hurston and Kennedy reported what they found to many people—the company itself, the local press, their bosses at the WPA—but nothing came of their protestations.

PAGE 60
Hurston had worked at numerous Black colleges throughout the '30s and '40s, usually as an English or drama professor (she much preferred teaching the latter), but her stays never lasted very long—a year at the most—since she wasn't much of a team player. So those who knew both Hurston and JAMES E. SHEPARD (1875–1947), founder and president of the North Carolina College for Negroes (now the North Carolina State University), knew her tenure there was doomed as well. NCCN was where nervous parents sent their children to keep them on the straight and narrow. (Shepard even maintained a strictly enforced "social hour," which was actually a *half* hour, and which was the only time of day that male and female students were allowed to talk to each other.) Initially the two of them got along quite well, but as time went by Shepard could no longer abide Hurston's wanton behavior (and her behavior *was*, by all accounts, fairly "wanton" during this time).

Meanwhile, Hurston was briefly married for a second time, in 1939, to a twenty-three-year-old student and WPA employee named Albert Price III (the forty-eight-year-old Hurston claimed to be twenty-nine on their marriage license). Not surprisingly, Hurston immediately regretted this decision, though they were not officially divorced until 1943. Back in the days before no-fault divorces, it was not uncommon for couples to make wild accusations in order to obtain one, and these two were no exception, with Hurston describing herself as "the meek and humble type," and thus utterly at the mercy of his drunken rages and Price accusing her of infecting him with a venereal disease, as well as of threatening him with voodoo curses (pretty funny if the latter were true!). Though a more recently discovered letter revealed that Hurston had, by the end, come to truly despise the man.

But the romantically impulsive Hurston wasn't through with marriage quite yet! In January of 1944 she got married yet again—this time to someone named James Howell Pitts, a Cleveland-based pharmacist—or was he Georgia-based? Who knows! Nor does anyone know *where* they met, or how. The license lists Pitts as being forty-five years old, so he at least was reasonably age-appropriate for the then fifty-three-year-old Hurston (who listed *her* ever-elastic age as forty on the same document). By October of that same year they were divorced, which also finally marked the end of her marrying career.

ABOVE
*Ethel Waters.*

PAGE 61
By 1941, ETHEL WATERS (1896–1977) was the highest paid performer on Broadway, and occasionally headed west to reenact some of her stage roles for the big screen. The survivor of an insanely dysfunctional childhood, Waters quickly went from being a top-billed nightclub singer to a top-selling recording artist before becoming a Broadway star. Later in life, as her fame began to wane, this self-styled "Catholic" became a born-again Christian, and toured regularly with evangelist Billy Graham as part of his "Up With People" crusades.

As was the case with her friendship with Fannie Hurst, the socially fluid Hurston never once exhibited the slightest envy for her friend's enormous success, and in fact gloried in it, along with Waters's larger-than-life personality (which most of their contemporaries would describe as overbearing).

Raised in a booze-free environment, Hurston never had much use for alcohol, let alone recreational drugs, and she grew increasingly intolerant of people who overindulged in either as she got older. Hurston's one vice was tobacco, and she smoked like a chimney throughout her adult life.

PAGE 62
Based on the comments Lippincott edited out of *Dust Tracks*, Hurston had a curious reaction—as well as an extreme one—to world events leading up to the US's involvement in WWII. She was in no way an admirer of totalitarian regimes like Nazi Germany or Imperial Japan (let alone Communist Russia), but the propaganda being churned out by the US government and its allies enraged her, what with all of their hypocritical talk about "freedom" and "democracy," while her own people were barely afforded either here at home. Thus she zeroed in on the many cultural and imperialistic crimes committed by the "Anglos" (a catch-all phrase meant to include, one would assume, both the English and American empires) over the prevailing centuries against people of color, and written with such rage that it's easy to see why it gave her publisher pause, even if that rage was justified. Lippincott surely did Hurston a favor by excising this tirade from her autobiography (which was released just as many of her countrymen were marching off to their certain deaths), though it also most likely put the first bee in her bonnet to start looking elsewhere for a publisher.

Some lazy or malevolent editor at the *World-Telegram* was likely to blame for drastically altering the meaning of Hurston's words in that article being read from in panel three, since she recalled the reporter she spoke to as being honest and sympathetic. Still, Hurston's worst experiences with racism all occurred in the North—where, since such incidents weren't government-imposed, she could *only* interpret as being entirely personal.

Hurston was well aware that "the freedom to live with your own kind," would extend to white people as well, and this is where she continually hit a wall when talking to liberals. But her point was this: *of course* no one should be prevented from moving, let alone forced out of their home—either via redlining or through violence or threats thereof—simply because they chose to integrate into a certain neighborhood. But do not use the power of the state to force people to live among those they'd rather *not* be amongst, either. *Birds of a feather flock together:* this is a simple fact of human nature, and where and when it exists, *leave it be*. In the meantime, let's trust our fellow humans to sort these things out gradually and peacefully, and *on the ground*, rather than let the state rob us of our agency via "social engineering."

A driving motive behind this belief for her, obviously, was cultural preservation, but Hurston also believed in *unqualified* equality under the law, and as such was horrified by the ever-growing "special victim" status being bestowed upon Black people by liberal-minded whites (*and* Blacks), which she considered both demoralizing and dehumanizing.

The radio interviewer in panels five and six is visually based on the nationally syndicated talk show host Mary Margaret McBride. You can find a segment of her interview with Hurston on YouTube, though the sweet-natured McBride was far more interested in *zombies* than in race relations ("Please do tell us *more* about the zombies, Zora!"). You'll also get an earful of Hurston's stubbornly thick Southern accent—one that even an Ivy League education couldn't eradicate!

PAGE 63

ADAM CLAYTON POWELL SR. (1865–1953) headed Harlem's Abyssinian Baptist Church, which under his leadership had over 10,000 members. He also cofounded the National Urban League, and had his hand in almost every major Black institution of his day.

ADAM CLAYTON POWELL JR. (1908–1972), was, for both good and for ill, something of a role model for the likes of the Reverends Jesse Jackson and Al Sharpton: early on he organized effective boycotts, and fought for (and achieved) equal public employment for Black people in New York City, yet he later devolved into an influence peddler, a shakedown artist, and an unrepentant skirt-chaser. Being the first African-American elected to congress since Reconstruction in 1944 made him an instant (and semi-permanent) hero amongst his people, yet his congressional legacy is also mixed: he was a brave and relentless crusader for civil rights legislation on the one hand, yet also a guy who *rarely showed up for work* on the other, and his abysmal attendance record (along with his profligate pilfering of public funds) led to his fellow Democrats voting to "exclude" him—in effect, *kicking him out* of Congress—in 1969. (He was reelected anyway, and his exclusion was later declared unconstitutional.) Though initially in the minority in her assessment, Hurston had Powell Jr. pegged as a man of poor character from the get-go. It must have been those *beady little eyes* of his!

ABOVE
*(L) Adam Clayton Powell Jr., and (R) his 1946 opponent, Grant Reynolds.*

Powell's 1946 opponent, GRANT REYNOLDS (1908–2004) also had an impressive civil rights record, in that this former army chaplain and attorney was later a leading force in the successful fight to end racial segregation within the US Armed Forces (which went into effect in 1948). This congressional campaign was Reynolds's first and last attempt to run for office.

Prior to the Great Depression and the New Deal, African-Americans used to overwhelmingly vote Republican, "the party of Lincoln." And even as late as 1946 the vote in Harlem was still roughly split fifty-fifty, which is why Hurston and others thought Reynolds stood a good chance of winning. Alas, the personality cult surrounding Powell Jr. proved to be insurmountable, both in this election and for decades to come.

PAGE 64

By this time Hurston had developed an odd friendship (though weren't they *all* odd?) with a character named Fred Irvine: a Miami-based Jewish expat from England who made a living chartering his ship to anyone for any reason, legal or illegal, moving people and/or cargo throughout the Caribbean. Hurston would occasionally accompany him on his voyages, though their relationship was strictly platonic (he was white, after all; plus, he *literally* had a girl in every port). After regaling Hurston with tales of Honduras's exotic Mayan interior, the two of them made plans to explore it together—only Irvine backed out at the last minute, leaving Hurston on her own, and with limited funds.

MAXWELL PERKINS (1884–1947) was renowned as the "discoverer" and editor of the likes of Hemingway, Fitzgerald, and countless other literary legends, so Hurston was understandably honored to suddenly find herself working with him—and just as understandably devastated by his sudden death. However, she did enjoy a good working relationship with Perkins' replacement, Burroughs Mitchell, though for reasons covered in the following pages she wound up writing only one book for him and Scribner's, which also proved to be her *last*.

That book is called *Seraph on the Suwanee*, and it's unique for several reasons, but primarily because it's about white people—and more specifically, *Southern* white people. How this came about is twofold: one was her aforementioned determination to write such a book just to *prove* she could (especially since countless white writers had previously written books about Black people, and Hurston even *liked* some of them). Also, during her many travels throughout the South, Hurston couldn't help but notice that white Southerners had their own colorful way of speaking—naturally similar to the Black dialects she was intimately familiar with, yet with its own distinct flavor nonetheless. Thus she began to jot down a new set of notes, and decided to put those notes to good use (I should also add here that Hurston strongly identified with the South in general, and as a Floridian in particular, and as such felt a strong cultural attachment to *all* of her native state's peoples).

Hurston also got "out of her skin" with this tale in more ways than one, in that the female protagonist, Arvay Meserve, could not possibly have been more different from Hurston. Throughout most of the book, Arvay is shown to be small-minded, bigoted, pessimistic, *terrified* of change, and utterly incapable of making a decision—thus empowering her husband, the ambitious, gregarious yet chauvinistic Jim Meserve ("Me Serve," get it?) even more than he was from the start. Eventually, Arvay develops a latent appreciation for her husband, and thus fully embraces him—which makes perfect sense within the context of the story, but sure doesn't resemble any other Hurston theme I can think of, let alone a feminist one. In fact, one could almost describe *Seraph* as being the polar opposite of *Their Eyes Were Watching God*.

*Seraph* is also more carefully edited than Hurston's previous books—which, while making it a smoother read, also makes it sound less...well, *Hurstonian* overall. It also makes one wonder if Lippincott had a point after all with his "hands off" policy regarding Hurston's work. Still, and as always, it's an utterly fascinating book, and highly recommended.

PAGE 65 AND 66
Hurston's accuser, a ten-year-old boy named Billy Allen, was the son of Mayme Allen, whom Hurston briefly rented a room from in 1946 while working for the Reynolds campaign. After Mayme caught her son engaging in homosexual acts with his friends, the boy began frantically accusing every adult he could think of whom his mother had an issue with of corrupting him—including an elderly janitor who, unlike Hurston, could not make bail, and spent the duration of the case in jail. (Hurston's bail and legal costs were covered by her new publisher, Scribner's, though they later deducted those fees from her royalties.) Mayme was allegedly trying to get her deeply troubled son committed at the time—and if so, most likely was also trying to build up her case while simultaneously deflecting blame from herself.

The biggest villain in this sordid tale, however, was one Alexander Miller, who represented the New York Society for the Prevention of Cruelty to Children (an organization that still exists—and who, at least in 1948, had way too much pull with the NYPD). This social justice crusader was so caught up in his cause that he not only had absolutely zero interest in Hurston or anyone else's innocence, but was more than willing to *invent* evidence and destroy peoples' lives in the process if that's what it took to save "just one child"—even if that child was a lying little sociopath like Hurston's accuser.

The boy and his friends' stories fell apart immediately once someone who *wasn't* Alexander Miller bothered to interview them, but Hurston's future and reputation was in limbo for months in the meantime. To make matters worse, a Black courthouse employee illegally sent sealed court documents about the case to various Black newspapers—including our dear old friends at the good old *Baltimore Afro-American*, who had a field day with the story—not only by portraying Hurston as a convicted child molester even after she was cleared of all charges, but even by quoting passages from her new novel out of context to make her look like even more of a deviant.

*Meanwhile,* yet totally unrelated, some lunatic in Los Angeles that Hurston only met once decided to sue her over an auto sale gone wrong that she had no part of, and began calling both white and Black newspapers to accuse her of indecent exposure and of "peddling marijuana" in order to build up his case. He lost the case, of course, but even Hurston's lawyer, Louis Waldman, had a hard time *not* believing there wasn't some kind of conspiracy against her in play. Her lawyer also wanted to sue both the Children's Society and the *Afro-American* for libel, figuring she had a good case on both counts, but Hurston was too emotionally and financially drained to fight anymore.

But most traumatic of all was the sense of abandonment she felt by her former Black colleagues, most of whom she had still maintained friendly correspondences with up until that point. Many of them even still lived in New York, yet wouldn't bother to check in on her, let alone exhibit even an ounce of support. The poet Arna Bontemps later stated that they all "knew" she was innocent, but failed to explain why he or anyone else couldn't bother to tell *her* that. Most disturbing of all was a sniggering-sounding letter Langston Hughes wrote to Bontemps during the trial, regarding a "leading lady writer of color" who'd been arrested "on a charge that should hardly be written down." That two grown men whose own sexual preferences where technically illegal at the time would be talking this way about someone who had loomed so large in their lives is mind-boggling—unless that was *why* they were getting a twisted thrill out of her ordeal, i.e.: "welcome to *our* world." Who knows?

I also can't help but wonder if Hurston's actual sexual preferences may have played a role in the silent treatment she'd received. Needless to say, there's a world of difference between a ten-year-old boy and a twenty-year-old man, both legally and morally, yet the age differences between Hurston and most of her paramours did keep expanding, which in turn generated much gossip, and, well...people's imaginations can resemble sewers sometimes.

And Hurston probably wasn't wrong when she speculated about her politics being a factor, since by that time the Black literati—particularly with the strident newcomer Richard Wright at the helm—all but made up a solid bloc of hard-left groupthink, with Hurston alone boldly representing anything that even resembled an opposing point of view. So to see their one remaining ideological opponent vanquished—even if it wasn't on the field of actual ideas—must have delighted at least some of them.

And make no mistake: Hurston *was* vanquished, at least temporarily. She even seriously considered suicide for a while, until she decided that being dead wasn't her style. So instead, she hid in a remote basement apartment in the Bronx until she finished a few freelance jobs, settled up some loose ends, and—other than attending a tribute dinner for Ethel Waters a few years later—left New York for good, in every sense of the word. This event also spelled the end of her formally active love life, and it's easy to see how such a trauma could have wiped any notions of romance from her consciousness. This permanent move was no great loss for her, really. Hurston craved hot weather anyway, and the sight of bare winter trees never failed to depress her. One person who missed her terribly, however, was Van Vechten, who thereafter often asked mutual acquaintances "Where's Zora?" in his correspondences.

PAGE 67 Hurston's friend Fred Irvine's cargo ship proved to be just the ticket once she was back in Florida, since it gave her a chance to escape from everything until she could, in her own words, "endure the sight of a Negro" again. (Her recent ordeal temporarily confirmed her suspicion that most Black people really can't stand to see one of their own succeed, and will conspire worse than the most racist honky to drag that "uppity Negro" down.) But as always, the need to make a buck raised its ugly head again.

At this point I should point out that Hurston had what could most generously be described as a "casual" relationship with money. When she was flush, she spent and lent freely, yet when she was skint she wasn't above begging, borrowing, or even *stealing* to make it through the day. (Once, when in desperate need of subway fare, she admitted to taking a dime out of a blind beggar's tin cup, explaining to him that she "needed it more than he did" at that moment—and no doubt repaid blind beggars everywhere ten-fold afterward.)

The one time Hurston had enough cash in hand to invest in real estate, she made an *anti*-investment in the form of a houseboat instead—one that she actually used as a boat, chugging up and down Florida's Indian and St. John rivers at every opportunity. (Her first houseboat was aptly named *Wanago*, while the second was hilariously dubbed the *Sun Tan*.) All of this surely must have given her penny- *and* pound-wise brothers fits, but Hurston never really gave a damn what her brothers or anyone else thought of her spending habits.

Hurston was by now struggling with her weight, and besides needing the cash, she seriously hoped that domestic work might help her shed some pounds! (Her well-to-do employers, a Mr. and Mrs. Burritt, later made cameo appearances in 1980's *Caddyshack*, as a pair of elderly golf club members.)

Initially quite leery of the potential embarrassment the exposure from that newspaper story might bring, it actually led to a lot of freelance offers after it was picked up by the wire services.

When pressed, Hurston would describe herself as "probably" an agnostic, yet due at least in part to her upbringing she never spoke like one, and her writings—including her book titles—are chock-full of biblical references and spiritual wonder. She certainly believed in the *power* of faith (as well as having been witness to it), not to mention making frequent note of the important role religion and faith play in individual cultures.

LEFT
*Ruby McCollum during her 1952 trial.*

PAGE 68
RUBY MCCOLLUM (1909–1992) and her husband were successful numbers runners—a fact that did her little good at her trial, since whites and Blacks alike resented her for her extralegal wealth. And regardless of how or why she got involved sexually with her victim—the supposed "pillar of the community," Dr. Leroy Adams—one thing became clear after the trial: the guy was a real monster. (For example, when his best friend made him the sole heir to his estate, Adams immediately began plotting his murder!) If the facts regarding his true character had been allowed in evidence, McCollum's self-defense plea might have held sway. Instead, she was given the death penalty, after which Hurston contacted a white male journalist, William Bradford Huie, hoping he could use his white male access to at least learn of Ruby's whereabouts and condition. After years of being stonewalled himself, Huie finally did meet with McCollum, who by then had completely lost her mind. Yet thanks to his and Hurston's tireless advocacy, Ruby's death sentence was commuted, and she was transferred to a mental institution.

PAGE 69
Hurston (to this author's eye, anyway) increasingly exhibited a protective streak toward Black children when in the presence of white adults—seemingly fearing how, no matter how well-intentioned, any passing comment implying inferiority might affect their young psyches. (This also may have been yet another reason she reacted so strongly to Mary Barnicle on page 54.) When a friend suggested that integration could help dispel such old stereotypes as Black people "smelling," Hurston responded by saying that a lot of poor Black kids *do* smell!

Regardless, Hurston's own social fluidity during her final Florida years had become so streamlined that she flowed in-between white and Black society (even marching into white friends' front doors, which was still socially verboten back then) without blinking an eye. The fact that she was a senior by this time would account for why her behavior didn't cause *too* much consternation, but she still was a one-woman integration machine!

RIGHT
*Among the many projects Hurston worked on in her later years was the ethnologically correct "Sara Lee" doll, conceived of by an elderly white acquaintance of hers named Sara Lee Creech, and which was eventually marketed by the Ideal Toy Company (though they had to be strong-armed into it by Creech's friend, Eleanor Roosevelt).*

PAGE 70
The conventional wisdom regarding Hurston's last decade was that it was her second set of "lost years," a notion that was reinforced by the distance she kept from mainstream intellectual and academic circles. Yet she remained very busy and, for the most part, quite content during these years. In fact, nothing much had really changed with her, in that she still held many jobs—librarian, high school teacher, newspaper editor, etc.—and still routinely quit each one out of boredom or disgust. She also had a wide variety

of interesting friends, took part in many projects, and she still wrote constantly, with many essays published during this time, almost all of which dealt with current political and social issues.

The one thing Hurston couldn't accomplish was to get another book published. Scribner's turned down every manuscript and proposal she submitted, and she had no luck with any other publishing house. The problem seems to be that Hurston could no longer fully concentrate on any one project for a sustained period. Whether this was due to the lingering effects of her traumatic arrest, or simply due to old age—or both—is hard to tell. Either way, it actually didn't seem to distress her all that much.

Hurston had long been an amateur historian of antiquity, particularly of the Levant region, and she worked off and on for years on this King Herod project of hers. Unfortunately, we can't judge for ourselves whether this book was a "mess" or not, since most of it was inadvertently destroyed in a fire shortly after her death.

Landscape painter and Fort Pierce native A. E. "BEANIE" BACKUS (1906–1990) was renowned for his studio's "open door" policy, which served as both a school/home for younger artists, as well as impromptu "beatnik" parties (Hurston was a regular attendee of the latter). Backus also mentored many young Black landscape artists (most notably Albert Hair), who—unable to show their work in white-owned galleries—set up roadside stands to sell their wares to tourists, and thus became known collectively as "The Highwaymen."

Former New York based radio scriptwriter MARJORIE SILVER ADLER (1908–1992) relocated with her husband, Doug, to Fort Pierce in 1946 to manage a local radio station. She remained good friends with Hurston for the few remaining years of her life.

PAGE 71

After moving semi-regularly up and down East Florida's central coast, Hurston eventually settled down in Fort Pierce for the last few years of her life. DR. CLEM C. BENTON (1898–1982) developed a small bungalow community in Fort Pierce, and he was quite delighted to discover that one of his new tenants turned out to be a literary genius, after which they spent many evenings together talking about everything.

While Hurston more or less said she "didn't want to be a bother" as the reason she refused to live with any relatives, I took the liberty of putting into her mouth what surely must have been the *real* reason why that prospect was out of the question (in spite of the fact that her many nieces and nephews had all long adored their freewheelin' Auntie Zora, almost to the point of worship). She even refused to accept money or gifts from her brothers when they were offered to her.

Hurston suffered a stroke in October 1959, and was hospitalized briefly before being transferred to the dreaded "welfare prison," where she could barely function for the last few months of her life. Hurston wasn't even able to *write* for almost a year prior to this, and thus was penniless by this point. A second stroke on January 29, 1960, at the age of sixty-eight, proved to be the end of her.

LEFT
*Ever since Alice Walker installed a tombstone, Hurston's gravesite has continually been gussied up, while Fort Pierce, Eatonville, and other Florida locales all now have Zora-related landmarks, museums, and festivals. She's become a cottage tourism industry!*

PAGE 72

This page was inspired by Alice Walker's 1975 article, "In Search of Zora Neale Hurston." In that story, Walker recounts Dr. C. C. Benton's anger—followed by his mortification—when she informed him of the condition of Hurston's gravesite in what is now known as the Garden of Heavenly Rest, and is regularly mowed now that it's a tourist attraction. While it's not unheard of (though still weird) for cemeteries to go "out of business," the fact that Hurston's grave didn't even have a marker is highly suspicious. Her funeral was well attended, and many people—her relatives as well as her many wealthy writer friends—contributed enough money to cover all the expenses, so somebody dropped the ball somewhere (or, more likely, walked off with some of the proceeds). Anyhow, Walker's new marker (over what has never been *confirmed* to be her actual grave), reads: "Zora Neale Hurston: A Genius of the South."

WORKS BY ZORA NEALE HURSTON

(All the titles listed below are still in print, though I included just their original publishers and original release dates.)

*Jonah's Gourd Vine*. J. B. Lippincott, 1934.

*Mules and Men*. J. B. Lippincott, 1935.

*Their Eyes Were Watching God*. J. B. Lippincott, 1937.

*Tell My Horse: Voodoo and Life in Haiti and Jamaica*. J. B. Lippincott, 1938.

*Moses, Man of the Mountain*. J. B. Lippincott, 1939.

*Dust Tracks on a Road: An Autobiography*. J. B. Lippincott, 1942.

*Seraph on the Suwanee*. Charles Scribner's Sons, 1948.

SHORT STORY COLLECTIONS

*I Love Myself When I Am Laughing...and Then Again When I Am Looking Mean and Impressive: A Zora Neale Hurston Reader*. Alice Walker ed. The Feminist Press, 1979.

*The Sanctified Church: The Folklore Writings of Zora Neale Hurston*. Turtle Island, 1981.

*Spunk: The Selected Short Stories of Zora Neale Hurston*. Turtle Island, 1985.

*The Complete Stories of Zora Neale Hurston*. Henry Louis Gates, Jr. and Sieglinde Lemke eds. Harper Collins, 1995.

*Every Tongue Got to Confess: Negro Folk-Tales from the Gulf States*. John Edgar Wideman foreword and Carla Kaplan ed. Harper Collins, 2001.

LETTERS

*Zora Neale Hurston: A Life in Letters*. Carla Kaplan ed. Doubleday, 2003.

BIOGRAPHIES

(NOTE: New information about Hurston is constantly being uncovered, so each of the following titles add to—and occasionally contradict—the information contained in their predecessors. Still, all of these biographies are highly recommended, especially Boyd's thoroughly comprehensive tome.)

*Zora Neale Hurston: A Literary Biography*. Robert E. Hemenway. University of Illinois Press, 1977.

*Wrapped in Rainbows: The Life of Zora Neale Hurston*. Valerie Boyd. Scribner, 2003.

*Zora Neale Hurston's Final Decade*. Virginia Lynn Moylan. University of Florida Press, 2011.

Also highly recommended is the recent *Miss Anne in Harlem* (Harper Perennial, 2014), by Hurston's letters editor, Carla Kaplan. This book covers the role white women played in the Harlem Renaissance movement, and has extensive information on Fannie Hurst, Annie Nathan Meyer, and Charlotte Mason, while Hurston's name pops up constantly throughout. A truly fascinating read.

Alternative comic creator Peter Bagge is best known for the '90s comic series Hate, featuring the semi-autobiographical antihero Buddy Bradley, whose adventures have been collected in two volumes: *Buddy Does Seattle* and *Buddy Does Jersey*, both from Fantagraphics.

Bagge has also created three graphic novels: *Reset*, *Apocalypse Nerd* (both Dark Horse), and *Other Lives* (DC/Vertigo). The journalistic strips Bagge has done for *Reason* have also been collected into a book entitled *Everybody Is Stupid Except For Me* (Fantagraphics). More recently, Bagge has written and drawn a full-length biographical comic, *Woman Rebel: The Margaret Sanger Story* (Drawn & Quarterly), and a collection of short biographical strips entitled *Founding Fathers Funnies* (Dark Horse) in early 2016.

Peter Bagge lives in Tacoma, WA, with his wife Joanne and two darn cats.